*To all the wonderful children that
have inspired me over the years*

The SuperConfitelligent

Loving to Learn through Movement & Play

Denise C. Hornbeak, M.S., N.V.T., C.L.P., L.E.K.

Published by:
  PEAK Producers
  Publisher and Distributor
  Cardiff-by-the-Sea, CA
  info@denisehornbeak.com

ISBN: 978-0-9800134-0-5

Printed in China
  Spectrum Books
  2455 Bennet Valley Rd.
  Santa Rosa, CA 95404

Front cover design by Michael Robb and Tammie Stimpfel. Cover photo by Mrs. Patricia Lawyer, Kindergarten teacher for my son, Kevin. She captured his colorful creation with Parquetry blocks.

Dedication

This book is dedicated to

my loving husband, Tom,

for supporting my vision

with his boundless patience

and knowingness,

to my SuperConfitelligent son, Kevin,

for being Kevin

and to all parents and teachers

throughout the world

for their innate love of children.

Contents

Dedication ii

Acknowledgements v

Preface vi

Introduction vii

Chapter 1 Your Role As Teacher 1

Chapter 2 Brain Plasticity................................. 17

Chapter 3 Brain Inhibitors To Learning............. 29

Chapter 4 Reflexes As Foundational 45

Chapter 5 Movement Is The Link To Learning ... 61

Chapter 6 Making Sense Of The Senses.............. 77

Chapter 7 Guiding Your Child's Spirit............... 119

Chapter 8 Favorite Connecting Activities........... 133

Chapter 9 A Love Of Learning.......................... 149

PLTs 163

Endnotes 164

Index 173

Author Biography 178

Acknowledgements

My deepest gratitude is extended to the following people who each, in their own special way, made valuable contributions to this project:

Carla Hannaford, Ph.D., neurobiologist and international educator, and most importantly, my dear friend

Svetlana Masguotova, Ph.D. from Poland and Russia, world-renowned reflex expert

Beverly Peterson, Ph.D., *Jeffrey Anshel*, O.D., *Diana Hoppe*, M.D., *Harald Blomberg*, M.D. of Stockholm, Sweden

Gail and Paul Dennison, Ph.D., for developing the field of movement-based learning called Educational Kinesiology and the Brain Gym® program

Carol Ann Erickson, Jon Bredal, Isabel Cohen, Rita Edwards, Cecilia Koester, Eve Kodiak and The HANDLE Institute International - many thanks for your generosity in sharing activities from your workshops and/or books

Laura Belle Wynne, Caroline Hobson, Rose Harrow, Thaddeus Trahan, Theresa Routon, Bill Stratton, Tina Baker, Veronica Getskow, Chris Zeitler, Jeanne Belli, Jean Bowlus, Daphne Martino and Dana Hornbeak for your guidance and expertise

Kathleen Locher, Joanne Stress, Isabelle Fernandez, Sharon Westre, Jocelyn Belleza, June Heinz, Nadine Iba, Wendy Retzer, Tiffany Lena, Charlotte Palmer, Patricia Rendon, Marcelle Goldsmith Shaman, Libby Brandt and Natasha Gogin-Moses for your contributions as a mother and/or as a professional

Teresa Jache, for coaching the early stages; *Laura Willson* and *Virginia LeRossignol Blades* for masterful editing

Andrew Greb for spotting those hidden grammatical errors

Michael Robb and Tammie Stimpel for designing the book

Dominic Alessio and Colleen Gardner for your unwavering friendship and support and *Jan Hunt*, Ph.D., my pod sister

Marcy Foster for your comments that drew out one more key point and distinction for the book

The *Cardinale* Family- *Brenda*, *Keith*, *Ty*, *Cole* and *Brooke*, for lovingly being a part of our extended family

All the parents that permitted me to take pictures of their wonderful children

And to all my family and friends, too numerous to mention, that encouraged me to share the value of this knowledge and my experience.

Preface

Will your child have the physical, mental and emotional skills needed to succeed in school? What does it take to maximize your child's development before entering the school arena? Will your child be ready to sit still in the classroom all day? Will they be able to focus and learn in a curious and relaxed manner? Do you have the Primary Learning Tools to raise a happy, creative, integrated, independent, *fantabulous*, well-adjusted, spirited and *SuperConfitelligent* child?

Today's children live in an intense society filled with images of violence, unhealthy competition, hectic schedules, pressure to succeed prematurely, and unrealistic expectations to behave like miniature adults. Kids are kids and they need years of innocence for exploring, fantasizing and creating in a secure and nurturing environment. The challenges of raising children to succeed in this ever-changing, fast-paced world are significant. For the first time, parents are realizing they must actively and attentively prepare their children for school or risk years of struggle.

Understanding how the brain and senses develop in babies, toddlers and pre-school children and their relationship to the child's physiology is critical to preparing them for learning in school. What children experience in the early years of life becomes the irreplaceable foundation and springboard for success in school, sports and, ultimately, all aspects of life!

Babies don't come with an instructional manual! It is my vision for this book to become a must-have read and guide for every parent, relative, caregiver, teacher, therapist and educational kinesiologist!

Introduction

We are not instinctively savvy to the complexities of child rearing. No how-to guide is ever automatically given to parents as they excitedly bring their baby home from the hospital. Unless early childhood development is your specialty, the developmental stages of childhood are a new exploration and can be a frightening awakening as well as a reality check. While you may be feeling knowledgeable and in control in the workplace, you may suddenly become uncertain about what to do at home with your tiny, innocent newborn, who is your super-sponge.

Anyone who interacts with children, be they parents, grandparents, educators, psychologists, developmental vision therapists, physical and occupational therapists or speech pathologists will benefit from reading this book. Whether you are an expectant mother, or a caregiver of a two or four-year-old, or a concerned teacher of a child having difficulties adjusting in the classroom, this book will provide Primary Learning Tools on how best to prepare your child for the opportunities and challenges of school life. The insights offered will not be limited to any race, culture or socio-economic class. The information is based on the universal principle that every child grows in a similar fashion — needing food, water, shelter, sunlight, emotional nourishment and physical connection in order to flourish and grow like the seed that blossoms into the beautiful, colorful and unique flower!

Conception to nine years old is a defining period in your child's development. The foundation for optimum health, success and well-being is laid during this time. These early years tremendously impact the rest of their lives. The choice of whether children are physically active, exploring their world inside their home and outside in nature with their hands, mouth and whole body or left propped in a bouncer or on a couch to watch television, videos or play computer and video games will make a profound difference in their developmental growth.

Scientists have found that children who are developmentally ready tend to do better in school. Those who are not ready for kindergarten are more apt to struggle in school, repeat grades, require special education assistance, and drop out of school. National research indicates that virtually 50 percent (50%) of children entering kindergarten experience moderate to severe problems in making a successful transition into school.[i]

Typically, most parents have assumed that preparation is only on the cognitive level, primarily with the ability to count, to say the letters of the alphabet and to recognize the primary colors and shapes. The National Education Goals Panel (NEGP) has, since 1990, ascribed to a broader, multi-faceted definition that includes a child's emotional, social and physical well-being, in addition to cognitive readiness. The NEGP emphasizes five dimensions of children's school readiness:

1. Physical well-being and motor development
2. Social and emotional development
3. Approaches to learning
4. Language development
5. Cognition and general knowledge

Children must be balanced within all dimensions of their mind and body to be fully prepared for the challenges of formal education.[ii] Clear sensory messages travel from all parts of the body to the brain and back again in a loop. Blocks to a child's success are caused by interference in optimal communication between the brain and body. With proper learning tools, parents can facilitate the release of the physical, mental and emotional blocks that impair the child's peak performance.

Kids flourish when they are moving and playing. Children instinctively want to move because the sensation of movement nourishes their brain. Parents, relatives, caregivers, teachers and therapists have so many occasions to contribute to the enrichment of children. This preparation begins in utero and has an everlasting impact for the rest of their lives. It will be a time that serves their growth as an individual not only academically but also as a whole person, giving them a loving, strong and safe foundation to move forward into school, knowing that learning is one of life's most exciting and fulfilling activities. For that reason, this book focuses on *Movement and Play!*

Your role as
teacher

**"Parents provide the primary
playground for learning."**
– Denise C. Hornbeak

An Awakening Story

I recently went into my dentist's office for a cleaning and
the hygienist mentioned how she makes her son, who will be
going into the second grade, do two hours of schoolwork every
day throughout his summer "vacation," sitting still working on
six pages so that he will stay in the habit of doing homework. I
thought to myself, "Give the kid a break, he's only 6 years old!"

The mother went on to say how easy it was for her 4-year-
old daughter to sit still for hours doing "homework." I politely
commented, "You might want to have both your children take
movement breaks to refresh their mind and body. It isn't our
nature to hold our body rigid and still. Have them also look up
to the distance frequently to relax the eyes. It is very hard on
the eyes to be looking up close for extended periods of time.
Excessive near-point focus can even deteriorate distant vision to
the point of needing glasses."

What we don't realize is how much compensating these
children will have to do internally, especially with their eyes,
posture and nervous systems to cope with this unrealistic
demand. These compensations become habitual, lead to other
complications and symptoms, and take a great deal of energy
away from the act of learning. Simple, whole-brain learning

becomes stressful, inefficient and riddled with effort.

On my way out of the office I took a deep breath and reaffirmed to myself how desperately important this information is for well-intentioned, caring parents who want the best for their children and just need education, some learning tools and guidance to choose a better way.

Everyone around the world wants what's best for their children. And people do the best they can with what they know. But where do parents get the idea that they are required to push their children and force results beginning at an unusually young age to be successful? Perhaps from their own parents because most people end up parenting the way they were parented? From the media? Television and magazines are filled with commercials and advertisements about learning centers and getting your youngster into preschool early for that competitive edge. Is it from peer pressure or a cultural consciousness? Is it a fear-related reaction pattern? Is it old-school thinking? The old ways don't work with today's children. There are simple ways that you can prepare your child for kindergarten. This book will guide you through with Primary Learning Tools (PLTs).

Prenatal

There are literally millions of influences affecting a child long before starting kindergarten. They actually begin in utero during the nine months of the mother's pregnancy. Mother's emotions, the hormones running through her body, the foods she eats, her breathing, her daily activity, her heartbeat and her thoughts are all affecting the fetus and how the baby will develop.

For the purposes of this book, a "parent" includes the biological, adoptive or foster parent, a stepparent, a caregiver, a legal guardian or anyone who steps in to play the parental nurture-providing, guiding role. Whether you are a mother, a stepfather, a speech pathologist or a friendly voice in the supermarket, you ARE a Teacher in that instant to that child. Even if it is a fleeting moment of teaching kindness or building self-esteem with a "Wow, you did it!", you can significantly contribute to that child's process of acquiring confidence and self-esteem, guiding their spirit and defining their world.

There are literally millions of influences affecting a child long before starting kindergarten. They actually begin in utero during the nine months of the mother's pregnancy. Mother's emotions, the hormones running through her body, the foods she eats, her breathing, her daily activity, her heartbeat and her thoughts are all affecting the fetus and how the baby will develop. From a tiny embryo growing in mother's womb, to the grand entrance to the world, to Baby's first words, to Baby's first step, the journey has passed through many milestones. Much anticipation and preparation is involved at each stage and must continue with the same care and deliberateness if parents are to properly prepare their child for their first formal educational milestone.

Parents are a child's first teacher. From the moment they wake up and throughout the child's day, parents can create learning scenarios that develop new neuropathways that lay the foundation for years of learning with ease. Unfortunately, many parents do not mindfully prepare their children for kindergarten. Some consider it to be an extension of daycare or the responsibility of preschool. Some are too pressed with work requirements and time constraints. Some consider it "nature's course" rather than a conscious pre-planning.

However, starting kindergarten is a major step in the whole process of a child's education. That first day of school will forever be imbedded in a child's memory on a cellular level for a lifetime - the excitement, the fears, the new clothes, the new backpack and lunch bag, the separation from Mom, Dad, Nanny or another nurturer. So many thoughts have been rushing through his or her mind: Will the other kids like me? Will I like the teacher? Will I be scared? Will I be bored? Will it be hard? Can I do it?

Teachable Minutes

As our child's first teacher, and to make that first day joyfully memorable, let's take a look at those five or six years before kindergarten. This is a time filled with teachable minutes. Every moment with your child is an opportunity to expose them to a new experience. Whether you are making dinner or driving in the car, there's a chance for enrichment. When preparing dinner, I used to have my very young son on my back in a backpack and he would very curiously look around my head to watch what I was doing. I would call out, "Oh, look at this beautiful, delicious orange carrot," and "Oh my, isn't this tomato so juicy and red?" He was hearing new words and associating shapes with those objects and starting to connect specific colors with their named form. I would also cut a big cube of tofu into many little squares. He would watch me doing it while we would listen to fun, upbeat music. It was usually the end of a very full day and some fast tempo music was invigorating.

Communication skills are at the heart of the educational

experience. Children learn their speech sounds by listening to the speech around them, so being descriptive in conversation, storytelling and playful games like the following all enhance the developing brain that acquires speech and language skills easier before the age of five.

Playful Games

1. Whether changing baby, riding in the car, or crawling together, it's fun to make basic sounds like "puh, puh, puh" and "mmmmm," and pretend to be animals with a "baa, baa, baa."
2. Explore your tongue with the wee ones in various ways - being lizards and sticking your tongue straight out and bringing it back in and out; drawing circles and Xs with the tongue; swishing back and forth, up and down, and clicking. They are such imitators that their tongue will be wagging right there with you.
3. Enjoy sucking a thick shake or smoothie through a straw or licking ice cream cones together. Sucking and licking are precursors to human languaging.
4. "Baby"— Watching my 3-year-old friend, Brooke, playing with her mom, inspired this game called "Baby." Pretend to be the Baby and your three-or four-year-old pretends to be "Mommy" or "Daddy." As the child feeds you, act like you don't know how to lick or chew and have them show you. Let them be the teacher. They love it!
5. Encourage yawning with an infant and young child by yawning around them. Open your mouth wide and let a yawn come forth, sound effects and all. This is no time to be polite by covering your mouth. For an added benefit, massage the tempo-mandibular joint (TMJ) on both sides of the face while yawning to relax facial muscles and positively effect the vertebral and nervous systems.[1-1] As seen via ultrasound, big yawning begins in week 31 of gestation. This is important for speech development, otherwise speech will be delayed.[1-2]

Nurturing Story

After taking a Brain Gym® workshop that I facilitated, S.W. of Orange, California, shared encouraging news about her grandson, Jude, a toddler with autistic symptoms.
"He was about 2½ at the time and was not speaking. He had never said 'Mama,' 'Nana,' 'please,' 'up,' 'hi' or any of the words that children use when they first use expressive language. Within a week after starting

*Brain Gym procedures with me, Jude had already
started saying several words such as 'hi' and 'bye.' It
was uncanny how rapidly he progressed."*

*Seven months later, here is S.W.'s update on Jude
who has just turned 3 years old:*
*"He is communicating with words, never stops.
Also, he was 'toe walking,' an autism trait, and now
he absolutely never toe walks. I know that Brain
Gym should be utilized as an adjunct to these little
peoples' early intervention programs."*

Children know intuitively what they need and will ask for it.
We only need learn the tools and be present enough to hear their
intuition speak, whether it is in words or actions. Jude knows what
works for him and will put up his little legs and feet for the activities.
S.W. found some teachable minutes to make a difference.

Colors

It is easy to teach colors in the midst of life. When speaking to
your infant on a daily basis, include the color of the object within
your conversation. It doesn't matter if baby is lying down and about
to have his diaper changed. You can say, "Oh, I love these green
pants that Aunt Mimi gave you." "Here comes a gray cat." "Let's
play with the blue and white ball." "Let's go see the black dog."

Mathematics

I started teaching my son when he was very young about
numbers and fractions. Why not? Children absorb so much
information like a sponge. They are curious creatures wanting
to experience the adventures of life. Everything is new and
interesting to them. Counting is easy to teach in the course
of daily life. When putting cereal Os, pieces of carrot or peas
on the high chair table, I would count them adding one at a
time. "onnnnnnnnnee-twwwoooo-thrrrrreeeee." Once they can
talk, you can say, "What comes next?" and in their funny baby
language they will happily tell you "free" or "four."

Flossing teeth becomes a daily nighttime ritual at an early age
for healthy teeth and gums. What a perfect time to learn about
halves, quarters and eighths! When there are very few teeth in
the mouth, we floss the bottom half and then the top half. As
more teeth grow in, the child learns about quarters. After one
quadrant was flossed, I would say "one-quarter done" and then

we would proceed to "two-quarters," "three-quarters" and "all done." Two-quarters soon became one-half and eighths were explored, too! Anytime children can use their body to learn a concept they will learn it more easily. We are all kinesthetic learners. We learn best by experiencing with our bodies.

My son Kevin wanted a fish for a pet, so we got a beta fish. Feeding the fish every day and changing the water every two weeks was his responsibility. When it came time to taking two cups of the old water out and putting two cups of fresh, clean water into the fish bowl, another opportunity to learn about fractions arose. The plastic cup didn't fill up completely, so he decided to remove half a cup of water at a time. "How many times will it take?" I asked. "Four," he replied. As he continued, he was saying, "½, 1 cup, 1½ cups and 2 cups."

Potty Training

A simple way to potty train a toddler between 18 and 30 months is to have the child run bare buns for a few days. They can be wearing their hat, shirt, socks and shoes playing in the backyard and in the house, but no diaper. Today's diapers are so absorbent the child doesn't know when they are wet. Bare buns will give them the sensory input they need to receive the feedback necessary to know when it's time to go to the toilet and when they have made an "Oops!"

> ### It's a big deal
>
> ▶ Do make a celebratory, big deal about the process of potty training. It is one of the rights of passage.

Accidents are bound to happen a few times, but if you can keep the tone of your voice kind and gentle, your child will not associate going to the bathroom with an upsetting experience. When my son, at age two, accidentally piddled on the new hardwood floor, I consciously chose not to scream even though that reaction did surface. I calmly said, "Oops, accidents happen, we just want to clean it up as quickly as possible." We went to get a paper towel and mopped it up together.

Do make a celebratory, big deal about the process of potty training. It is one of the rights of passage. Bring a special child-size toilet into the bathroom. It will be his/her very own "big girl" or "big boy" toilet. For boys, Cheerios® are fun to use as a target in the pot. I would bring the portable toilet along in the car so he could answer the urge promptly, even if it meant pulling over to the side of the road! With each passing day your child will feel proud of their accomplishments. As parents you will feel really proud and relieved with another milestone achieved. Imagine all the money you will save not needing to buy any more diapers!

Penmanship

Reading and writing difficulties have become so prevalent today for many children because we have put the cart before the horse. The young child is not given sufficient opportunity to write before he is faced with the printed page. From a historical and developmental standpoint, this is quite out of step. The very act of writing, the physical movements involved, prepares the body in large part for those subtle eye movements which have to be accomplished in a matter of split seconds during reading and absorption into consciousness. The movements during reading are the fruits of the writing skill. Attention to detail and practice of writing must come first.

Penmanship does not have to be an ordeal for children. (Let's not keep tears the norm.) Readiness for handwriting requires the development of specific skills of the physical body.

> ### Writing-Prep activities
>
> • Crab
> • Loopty Loops
> • Snowballs
> • Evolving Art
> • Lazy 8s
> • Talking Hand Motions
> • Pencil Grip

The child must first develop postural control in order to sit correctly and comfortably in a chair with strong muscle tone of the core muscles. Otherwise they will slouch or fidget without the ability to focus. They must also have sensory integration and be accepting of light touch to hold the pencil or crayon or whatever tool they are using. It is important that the neck and shoulders are relaxed so that the child doesn't stressfully use the whole arm, shoulder, hand and fingers, causing a tight grip and unnecessary pain. Other essential skills are finger strength and dexterity, spatial orientation, the ability to cross the body's central midline and the visual skills of eye-hand coordination, eye-vergence balance, eye teaming and tracking.[1-3]

Teachable-Minute Activities for Ease of Writing

1. Crab – 1½ to age 99 with your children, grandchildren and great-grandchildren – Squat down and lean back so only hands and feet are touching the ground or carpet. You are in supine position with stomach facing up. Tighten the "tummy muscles" and lift opposite limbs so one hand can touch the opposite thigh, knee or foot. Then have the other hand touch the opposite leg. Repeat this pattern walking like a crab forward and back. That burning sensation is those core muscles strengthening. Burn baby, burn! The Crab strengthens the core muscles of the abdominal area for postural control and at the same time activates both hemispheres of the brain for whole-brain functioning.

▲ **Three boys doing the crab**

2. Loopty Loops – Two to age 99 – draw a row of loops like many lower case cursive e's connected and then hand the pad of paper to your child inviting them to copy the loops below yours.

It looks like this:

eeeeeeeeeeeeeeeeeeeeeeeeeeeeeeee

You can also draw a row of cups:

uuuuuuuuuuuuuuuuuuuuuuuuuuuuu

or a row of big loops:

eeeeeeeeeeeeeeeeeeeeeeeeeeeee

or a row of tepees:

Chapter 1 Your role as teacher

or a row of c's:

It looks like ocean waves, or you can vary it for double waves.

Variations: For variety and if age appropriate, have the child say the directions as they draw the formations - up, around, down, in, right, left - experiencing these vertical and horizontal spatial dimensions.

More variations: The loops can be drawn upside-down in a row and/or combined together, e.g., little loop, big loop, little loop. Let your imagination go wild! Also encourage your child to make a pattern across a row for you to imitate. They love that too!

Drawing Loopty Loops is a precursor to writing. This activity is extremely useful to entertain a child before or after a meal in a restaurant or especially in a place where it is most appropriate to be quiet, e.g. library, church or even on an airplane.

Nurturing Moment

– Tiffany, a mother from Carlsbad, California

"I was traveling with Mikey, age 6, and Joey, age 4, to Florida for vacation. They were getting a little antsy on the plane and I pulled out some paper and pens to occupy them but they didn't want to draw pictures. I started having Mikey identify random written numbers--6, 49, 270, etc., but of course, Joey was too young to read the numbers. I remembered how you had occupied Joey at our YMCA meeting by drawing the curly cues (Loopty Loops) and abstract designs and having him copy them, so I tried that with him, and to my surprise, he really enjoyed it and kept saying, 'Do another one, Mom!' "

3. Evolving Art – Two to age 99 – This is another great activity for a restaurant before or after the meal or on a bus or airplane. With two or more people, have one-person start with a blank piece of paper and a crayon, pencil or marker drawing a shape, squiggly or letter. Pass it to the next person to add their piece to the first form. Each person adds a little more as the paper is passed around and around until everyone has added all they want to the evolving artwork. The end result is spectacular and far more beautiful than what would have come out of one mind. Once it is complete, the group names the piece of art, and everyone has learned the value of collective creating.[1-4]

4. Snowballs – Two to age 99 – Have your child take a piece of white paper (8½ X 11" works great), hold it vertically and tear ½" to 1" strips. Next use one hand to crunch each strip into tiny little white balls. (Of course if the child is a 2 to 4 year old, he may want to use both hands.) After all 8-10 "snowballs" have been made, count them all homolaterally with first one hand and then the other, and then counting the first "snowball" with one hand and the second one with the other hand, alternating until all "snowballs" are counted. When finished, put each "snowball" in a bag or bowl by picking up the first one with the thumb and index finger, second one with the thumb and middle finger, third one with the thumb and ring finger and fourth one with the thumb and pinky. Repeat the sequence until all balls are put in the container. An entertaining variation is to flick each ball across a table or in the air into a trashcan. Snowballs develop finger and hand dexterity and prepare fingers for proper pencil grip.[1-5]

▲ Snowballs develop finger and hand dexterity and prepare fingers for proper pencil grip.

Here are more suggestions for ease of writing because this is such a big issue in many homes especially at homework time. I never made the assumption that because Kevin is a boy, he would have a hard time writing and it would be messy. Boys do not automatically have poor penmanship. Boys can develop the ability to write their thoughts on paper in an organized, neat fashion. It all starts in the early years with movement patterns and the coordination of the body.

More Activities to Prepare for the Skills of Writing

1. Lazy 8s – The basic form starts in the middle lined up with the midline of your body, moves up to the left, around, down and crosses in the middle before moving up and around to the right. **Lazy 8s in the air** — When doing the Lazy 8 in the air, first hold your nondominant thumb sticking up directly in front of the middle of the body and move it up to the left in the basic form. The pattern is repeated at least three times with the eyes  following the thumb in the lazy 8 pattern around and around. Then switch to the dominant hand and then both hands clasped together with the thumbs making an X. You can also make them on big and small paper with pencil, pen, crayons, colored pencils, markers, paint, etc. A tasty option is to trace the Lazy 8 with chocolate pudding or whipped cream on the kitchen table.

Variation: First make the Lazy 8 big enough to fill a letter-size piece of paper, then progressively smaller as you fold the paper in half after making Lazy 8s with one hand, then the other, then both hands at each new size of smaller paper. When the paper has become too small to fold, open it up and hold it in your writing hand with arm hanging by your side. Then with that hand only, crunch the paper into a little ball for hand flexibility and dexterity and throw it into a trash can an appropriate distance away for eye-hand coordination.

Nurturing Moment

KDH was reversing his S's at age five. I had him do Lazy 8s a few times and bingo, he did it correctly. The following day when he went to write an S without having done the Lazy 8 since the day before, he wrote it backwards and quickly recognized that it was wrong and self-corrected it! He never reversed his S after that.

2. **Talking Hand Motions** – In the midst of play have hands move through the Grasp reflex patterns as illustrated on **page 13** by Dr. Svetlana Masgutova of Poland. You can make it into a creative, fantasy activity, imagining what the different animals or objects are saying.

3. **Pencil grip** – Make up a fun story to illustrate the best pencil grip to use. The key points are the bent thumb and index finger are the grasping claws and the other three fingers support them. My favorite description is from Marcelle Goldsmith Shaman, an occupational therapist from Cape Town, South Africa.

Hot Dog Story: "Explain to the child that the pencil is the hot dog or sausage or tofu pup; the index finger (pointer finger) is the top of the bun, therefore on top of the pencil shaft; the thumb is the bottom of the bun (bottom of pencil shaft) and the middle finger is the plate on which the hotdog rests (pencil rests on middle finger). The middle phalanx (joint) of the index finger is flexed (bent), while the last joint is extended (straight). I explain this in a few ways. Either it's a carrot decoration on the top of the bun, or it looks like a mountain peak (in Cape Town, I often use the reference of the mountain we see from our area, called Devil's Peak--the peak of the index finger on the pencil."

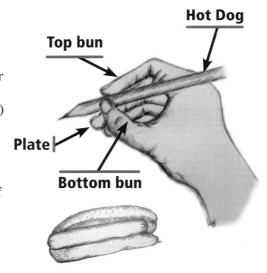

Hot Dog

Top bun

Plate

Bottom bun

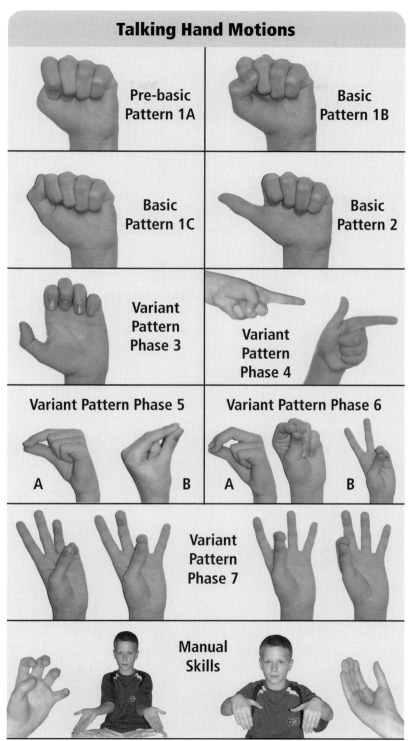

Talking Hand Motions

Pre-basic
Pattern 1A

Basic
Pattern 1B

Basic
Pattern 1C

Basic
Pattern 2

Variant
Pattern
Phase 3

Variant
Pattern
Phase 4

Variant Pattern Phase 5

A   B

Variant Pattern Phase 6

A   B

Variant
Pattern
Phase 7

Manual
Skills

Revealing Moment

– A week after learning this grip, Barbara Wells had this comment:

"Changing my grip has made writing easier. The pen in my hand feels fluid instead of tight and jerky when I write. I used to only get a sentence written in cursive before my hand cramped and I felt tension in my arm and neck. With the new grip I feel no cramping in my hand or arm thus I can write longer. Amazing something so simple can make such a huge difference."

4. Chalk and Jumbo Crayons – Use big chalk and jumbo crayons for lots of fun drawing, writing and doodling.

Key PLT for Beautiful Penmanship

I found the **Loopty Loops** on **page 8** to be the one key, fun Primary Learning Tool to do with my son in the early years that made the biggest difference in his ease of writing beautifully. It has always been a joy to look at both his cursive writing and printing. For more activities, especially for your children who are school age and still struggling with penmanship, see the writing section of Isabel Cohen and Marcelle Goldsmith's practical, user-friendly photo manual, *Hands On: How to use Brain Gym® in the Classroom.*[1-6]

Quality Time

Today's parents are busy maneuvering the basic physical needs of the household—cooking, cleaning, laundering, shopping—and quite often do so while talking on their cell phone. What's the message being sent to our children?

Many parents and caregivers are using the television, video games and/or the computer to baby-sit children and keep them occupied and entertained. Electronics have become the new occupational babysitter. While most parents would agree this has provided short-term benefit, it has not been without a long-term price. There is no substitute for human interaction. Whatever time you have with your child, make it a personal, focused, connecting and nurturing moment.

Nurturing Moment

I saw a lady with her 2-year-old daughter and 5-year-old son the other day at the pool. I was delighted to see her doing the "Hokey-Pokey" in the water with her daughter. Mom was holding her while singing the song and following the prompts – putting her right hand in, pulling her right hand out and putting her right hand in and shaking it all about. What a learning opportunity! The young girl was learning about these things that stick out from the body called "hands" and "feet." And she was learning about the concepts of "in" and "out." And she was having the vestibular stimulation of buoyancy and spinning in the water. She was learning about her rights and her lefts. And most of all she was experiencing joy, playing and bonding with Mom!

There is no question it takes a lot of energy and patience to raise children. That means planning our time wisely and acknowledging when we need to take a pausing moment for ourselves. I am not afraid to let those around me know that I am in a cranky mood so they know it is normal to have different feelings, and then I model what to do about it. After a pausing moment of even just a minute, I can return refreshed and ready to practice patience once again.

Nurturing Moment

So many stages of Kevin's development, I believe, have been smooth because I took the TIME in our very full lives to let him explore whatever drew his curiosity. When he was 1½ years old, we spent a month going to the kitchen tool drawer, taking out a screwdriver and batteries, and removing the screw from one of his toys to replace the batteries. Over and over, every day for a month we repeated the ritual. It's no surprise one of his first words he said was "stewdiva." It took a lot of patience on my part, but the rewards will last a lifetime; Kevin developed incredible eye-hand coordination, has the focus and persistence to stay on task, and he has engineering skills that now surpass his father's!

"You are not the only influence in your children's world, so be the best influence!"

— Dr. Phil McGraw

Brain plasticity

> ## "We cannot always build the future for our youth, but we can build our youth for the future."
>
> — Franklin D. Roosevelt

What can we do to facilitate our children in reaching their full potential?

When a few parents in the Cardiff School District heard that my son had earned the maximum Advance score, 600 out of 600, on his STAR testing (California's Standardized Testing and Reporting program) in Math in the second grade, they approached me to work with their children. I enthusiastically said "Yes," and proceeded to create the Be a STAR Tester workshop, which included simple Brain Gym® movements that could be done before and during testing. Brain Gym is a movement-based program that enhances learning and performance in all areas of daily life. The Brain Gym program began in the 1970s with the work of two educators: Dr. Paul Dennison and Gail E. Dennison. Initially, the Dennisons were seeking more effective ways to help children and adults who had been identified as "learning disabled" access more of their full potential. Brain Gym is the core program of Educational Kinesiology (Edu-K), the study and application of posture and movement to enhance academic, interpersonal and physical learning.[2-1]

One of the parents who participated in the workshop with two of her sons excitedly came up to me after we had received the test results to inform me that she was very pleased with the outcome. Her son Nathan had raised his Math STAR testing score 174 points from second to third grade and he had improved his English-Language Arts score 20 points. This was a 29% increase in Math. He actually scored 600 correct out of a possible 600.

His mother revealed,

"More importantly, last year Nathan placed slightly below the Mean Scale Score in both areas and this year he scored significantly above the Mean, especially with his perfect math score."

She was equally proud of her other son.

"As for Skip, I just didn't know what to expect with it being the first time he would be taking any sort of standardized test. All I know is that in comparing my children, he is the less focused of the two. His reading skills and comprehension are not that of my older child. I wouldn't have been surprised had he performed lower than my other child did in second grade. I was quite pleasantly surprised when Skip scored well into the Advanced Level for both English and Math. Apparently, with the help of Brain Gym Activities, he is able to focus when it comes time to test!"

Another mother who attended the workshop happily reported that her son also achieved a perfect score on the STAR testing in Math for fourth grade.

The final clincher to this STAR testing story is that my son repeated his 600 out of 600 Math test score in the third and fourth grades - 100% correct - as he did in the second grade. He also scored again in the Advanced level in English-Language Arts.

I am thrilled for these students and for their parents. Their knowledge of mathematical facts was easily accessed, so they succeeded under testing conditions. This was our intention during the Be a STAR Tester workshop. Learning is supposed to be fun and testing can be another exciting game. It is all in our perception.

The 100% score is truly amazing! What's even more amazing is the fact that these young boys were able to think clearly and consistently, and to focus successfully on testing for four days straight. That's what I call impressive!

Are these children inherently gifted? Or does movement reorganize the brain?

For many years scientists have debated the nature versus nurture theory. Is it genetics or the environmental exposure to caring people throughout a child's life? The controversy is over the extent to which genes influence intelligence compared to the effect of the environment in the early years of child rearing as well as during formal education and from the child's culture. Whether parents believe that nature or nurture plays a greater role in the outcome of their child's intelligence and their talents will dramatically influence and determine how they decide to raise our future leaders.

Nature vs. Nurture

▶ Genes account for an estimated 50% of a person's intelligence and the other 50% is environmental factors.

Some people believe that a child's intelligence comes from the maternal side of the family and it's "a done deal." Others believe that keeping the mind active and learning during pregnancy will have a significantly positive effect on the newborn's intelligence. Others will play Mozart music for its prenatal benefits.

Couples today are going to greater lengths to bring a child into the world, to become parents and to create a family nucleus. Conceptions are taking more forms than ever before. A baby may be conceived "through the miracle of modern science" via an egg or sperm donor, artificial insemination, and/or surrogacy. And adoptions continue to make a statement in favor of the nurture theory.

From conception, heredity has already played its part in determining how smart a child will be. Scientists in the field of behavioral genetics estimate that genes account for 50% of a person's intelligence. The highest correlation is with subjects who are identical twins. Those twins raised together have a 0.86 correlation between their IQs. The other 50% of a person's intelligence is a result of the fast moving neural transmissions created from environmental factors, the most important of which occur during pregnancy. Up to twenty percent (20%) of the IQ variance is from the prenatal period.[2-2] A key point, which will be explored in much greater detail in the next chapter, is the exposure to stress during pregnancy. Stress is unavoidable, but it can be managed so that adrenaline and cortisol levels stay at a minimum while the embryo and fetus develop. These stress hormones will play their role to signal an ensuing birth but must be kept in check during the nine months.

Genes program the sequence of neural development. The nervous system matures in a programmed sequence from the bottom of the spinal cord at the tailbone to the head, as with the evolution of all vertebrate species. At birth, the spinal cord, the pons and the medulla of the hindbrain, with their vital functions of survival, growth and bonding, are almost fully developed. The cerebellum and midbrain begin myelinating subsequently. For the first 18 years after birth, the neocortex is under construction and, interestingly, some researchers find the prefrontal cortex continues to develop until death. Although this sequence of neural development is genetically programmed, the quality of that development is shaped by environmental factors.[2-3]

Study

► Lack of stimulation and social isolation stunts a child's emotional, sensory, motor and linguistic development.
— Spitz series comparing two disadvantaged groups

Researchers have studied the effects of environmental factors such as nurturance, attention, encouragement, discipline and opportunities. Studies like the famous Spitz series comparing two disadvantaged groups, babies of prison mothers raised in a nearby nursery and babies raised in an adequate foundling home, demonstrate how early nurturing and sensorial stimulation are essential to child development. The prison mothers lavished their babies with enormous affection and attention. Despite the institutional setting and the limited contact with their mothers, these babies developed normally. The orphans, by contrast, were left isolated with minimal stimulation. Many did not survive to their second year. Most subjects were unable to walk and talk at age three, their physical growth was stunted, and they were mentally retarded, apathetic and withdrawn. The results changed adoption policies. Lack of stimulation and social isolation stunts a child's emotional, sensory, motor and linguistic development.[2-4]

Today's neurobiologists view the brain as almost as malleable for the elderly as for our youth. The mature human brain has the potential for neuronal regeneration. Although the blood, heart, liver, kidneys, lungs and skin can all regenerate new cells to replace damaged ones, until recently scientists believed that such plasticity did not extend to the adult central nervous system, which consists of the brain and spinal cord. It was thought that the brain, when damaged, could compensate by making new connections but could not repair its nerve cells. It was believed that the brain lacked the stem cells that would allow for neurogenesis.

Peter S. Eriksson of the Sahlgrenska University Hospital in Goteborg, Sweden, and Fred Gage at the Salk Institute for Biological Studies in La Jolla, California, discovered that the mature human brain with its 100 billion neuronal cells can regenerate new neurons routinely, especially in the hippocampus, an area of the midbrain important to memory and learning. It is this exact hippocampal area, identified as the dentate gyrus, where neuronal production had been found in adult rats as early as 1965, by Joseph Altman and Gopal D. Das of the Massachusetts Institute of Technology.[2-5]

Findings have confirmed that enriched environments do affect adult neurogenesis to the intricately-wired human brain. Applying technology which was not available in the 1960s, Gerd Kempermann and Fred Gage's group demonstrated in 1997 that adult mice given enhanced living conditions (including stimulation with different toys, social interactions with other mice, and choices of different foods) grew sixty percent (60%) more new granule cells in the dentate gyrus than did genetically-identical control animals. The big, complex environment provided greater room to explore their surroundings and to interact with others. The mice furthermore performed better on learning tests (for instance, they were more successful at learning to navigate out of a pool of water).[2-6]

> **Learning tests**
>
> ► Adult mice given enhanced living conditions performed better on learning tests.

After hearing these results, the neuroscientist Henriette van Pragg researched to determine the element of this enriched environment that was the most important. Some mice were put in a complex environment, some were trained to do certain tasks, some had minimal exercise and some had a running wheel placed in the cage so they had free access to voluntarily exercise. The most dramatic increase in cell proliferation was with the animals with the running wheel. They would run (actually, it's more like walking) six to ten hours a day. Having the running wheel virtually doubled the number of dividing cells. At the end of four weeks, it was discovered that the enriched environment did not increase the pool of dividing cells, but promoted greater survival of those cells, whereas running actually increased the entire pool. The same number of cells died, but the net effect was that the runners ended up with as many cells as the enriched environment group. And both groups nearly doubled the nerve cells of the control group.[2-7]

The running wheel gave them ample opportunity for cross-lateral activity, thus also influencing brain wiring in ways that enhance brain function, learning, faster acquisition and better retention.[2-8]

Dr. Lise Eliot also verified that the brain of a child is extremely malleable. As a neuroscientist, she studied in the field of neural plasticity how adaptable the brain can be when exposed to sensory and motor experience.

She states that all the neurons formed by week eighteen of the pregnancy can be molded with experience.[2-9] Children's neurological development will depend upon their unique life experiences.

Nurturing for Brain Growth and Plasticity

This book emphasizes the significant difference you as a parent can make through nurturance. The act of nurturing can make that difference and be playful. Something as simple as rolling a ball has benefits you may never have thought of. Simple nurturing moment activities like getting down on the floor with your child from an early age, cuddling, playing and rolling a ball or two back and forth can have a tremendous impact on their development. During such an activity, the child is experiencing movements of the whole body, especially the eyes, arms and legs, and that movement grows the brain. The contact with the child through touch can be comforting and calming to their nervous system. Speaking, especially in a patient, kind tone, opens their ears to the magic of language. And best of all, the laughter of play warms their heart and reassures and reaffirms to them how wonderful and lovable they are.

The early years of childhood are the prime time to create nurturing moments of quality experiences that enhance brain development. While in the womb, mother's movements promote fetal growth and development. After birth, babies sleep about fourteen hours a day and the rest of the time they are perfectly content nursing and being held close to mother to hear her heartbeat and gurgling sounds so familiar from the nine months prior in the womb. At three months, babies begin to respond more to the outside world and start to experience their separateness from mother.

Children develop their neural wiring in direct response to their life experiences. The human nervous system consists of about the same amount of neurons as there are stars in the Milky Way galaxy (10^{11} neurons). Each neuron has between 1,000-10,000 synaptic connections. Movement creates the intricate, nerve cell networks. As long as stimulation continues, more dendritic branches manifest. Interestingly enough, the cerebellum houses the neurons that have the most connections – linking movement to learning.[2-10]

What to do

• Make use of Baby's cues
• Become consciously aware and observe with wonderment
• Spend Tummy Time

We can dynamically encourage and facilitate the developmental stages. Nature will take its course when we provide the safe, loving environment. When Baby is on his/her tummy and moving and squirming, stand back and observe with wonderment all the coordination going into the movement. The body and brain work together to organize the body from its core to roll over. If your baby is moving in the attempt to roll over, their sounds may be your cue to come over and see what movements they are making. If it appears they have had a good workout for the morning, then perhaps it's time to pick them up or turn them over to see the world from a new perspective. Quite often, it will be their cry after the fact that catches your attention. They're telling you, in the best way they know how, they are ready for a change.

▲ **Tummy Time can take many forms!**

The child's inherent curiosity and innate desire to explore their world will provide the cues to their parents to encourage experiences that affect the many stages of development. Parents look with great expectation for that first smile and other big milestones like crawling and "Baby's" first step. Every child will provide many other cues like turning the head or lifting the head while on their tummy, or movement of the body in preparation for rolling over and subtle movements of the eyes.

Go with the responses of the infant. Make use of the auditory and visual stimuli that they are naturally drawn to or react to. When you see your baby turn their head towards the cat meowing, it is a wonderful opportunity to talk about the cat or carry the baby over to feel the soft texture of the cat's fur. Even a four-month-old can start experiencing their world in a safe, supervised environment. In actuality, they have been experiencing their world since the early weeks in utero.

Do we ever tire of watching our child peacefully sleep regardless of what age they are? How many parents love to watch their infant just lying there being or moving their arms and legs in the crib or on the changing table? Watching, noticing and marveling at

their child's beauty even when they are sleeping—sometimes especially when they are sleeping! Observing and becoming more consciously aware lets us appreciate the wonders of our creation!

I always marveled at the little things, the simple movements, and made use of my son's cues by turning

▲ **Angelic baby sleeping**

them into teachable minutes. When Kevin was three weeks old and kicking away on the changing table, I would say, "Kick, kick, kick, kick, kick, kick, kick!" I was putting a word to his action for him. "Oh, you are getting those feet and legs ready for soccer." Sure enough, he loves the sport.

Parents, from your newborn's birth, you can enjoy connecting moments. Having your baby rest on your tummy, skin-to-skin or even clothed, is a powerful bonding experience for both of you. Baby gets to hear your heartbeat, moves up and down with your breathing, and smells and feels your body. Your infant will also start building neck muscles by lifting their head. This is setting the stage for being able to hold their head up on their own. This will lead to many foundational skills and ultimately to sitting upright in a chair in a classroom using both eyes and ears actively to learn in school.

Indigo and Crystal Children

In examining the nature versus nurture controversy and how to appropriately prepare children in the 21st century for school and ultimately for life, there is a particular group of children needing to be addressed. Experts call them the Indigo and Crystal children.[2-11] Nancy Tappe, renowned philosopher, teacher, minister and author, was the first person to identify Indigo children and describe their behaviors.

The Indigo children phenomenon is one of the most exciting changes in basic human nature ever observed and documented in our society. It is an emerging pattern of human behavior affecting our children and our relationships with them. The theory is that they are very different than children from all of the previous generations throughout civilization. The change is in the inherent nature of their consciousness.

Give them

- Lots of Love
- Benevolent structure
- Conscious guidance
- Opportunities to display their uniqueness [2-13]

What is an Indigo Child? What sets him or her apart from any child of any other era? The Indigo child is a girl or boy who displays a novel and extraordinary set of psychological attributes.

They are creative, curious, passionate, energetic, and occasionally super sensitive, impulsive and distractible. Indigos can be very willful, temperamental and warrior-like in spirit; they frequently see other ways of doing things that are often a better way. They operate as though they have a clear, focused mission in life and express their determination to reveal to others "the other way" which is different from the old belief systems and patterns.[2-12]

The traditional approaches to parenting and education do not seem to be effective with these children. They have a unique difficulty with absolute authority. Telling them what they must do is ineffectual without giving them an explanation and choices. With their highly developed intuitive system, they understand far more than what is being said. They will question a belief system to the point that a parent, being introspectively honest, will also question its absolute nature. After an authoritative "This way or else," these children will genuinely insist "But why?" Responding with a knee-jerk reaction modeled by our parents or responding with "Because I said so!" simply doesn't work.

According to Nancy Tappe the following are the four basic simple needs of Indigos.

In fact, most of today's children were born to dissolve those old systems that no longer serve humanity. Those systems include belief systems, as well as educational, political and legal processes lacking integrity. We must STOP in the midst of a power struggle and ask ourselves, "As a parent, am I handling this situation from my old values-based system or from my heart in this present moment?"

Indigo children, with their excellent lateral thinking ability, see other ways of doing things that are often, quite frankly, a better way. They cannot be shamed into doing it your way or made to feel guilty with the threat: "Wait until your Dad hears about this!" Adults may succeed in making them feel badly in the moment, but these highly evolved souls know instinctively that this is not the way to be treated. Indigo children are here to show us what our world needs to release, for tomorrow to take place. It will take a great deal of patience, and an open mind and heart, to relate to these children. It is well worth every deep breath you take to "re-center" yourself to your inner peaceful place!

Indigo children seem to be clearing the way for the Crystal children. These Crystal children are even more spiritually sensitive than the Indigo children. They come without the warrior spirit and are thus much more open and much more vulnerable. According to Doreen Virtue, Ph.D., Crystal children, born around the year 1995 or after, are very powerful

Guiding Indigo and Crystal Children

- Create trust by being sincere
- Give them a Voice, one child at a time.
- Make your personal decision after listening and evaluating how it resonates with your true self
- Make statements like "I need you to cooperate during _____."
- Ask questions to find out where the child is coming from.
- Examine their point of view.
- Let them express appropriately their emotions.

beings. Like the Indigo children, their purpose on this earth is to advance human evolution on the spiritual level. They, too, are here to teach man his divinity and inner power, although they do not have the fiery temperament and intense determination of an Indigo child. The Crystal child, following the path of the trailblazing Indigo child, is a powerful force of peace and love for all mankind.[2-14]

From Dr. Virtue's perspective, many of the Indigo and Crystal children are being misdiagnosed and mislabeled. Some Indigo children are thought to be ADD (Attention Deficit Disorder) or ADHD (Attention Deficit with Hyperactivity Disorder). A number of adults want them medicated so that they conform to society at the expense of their sensitive, intuitive and willful selves. Dr. Virtue's more apropos description of the acronym ADHD is a child who has Attention Dialed into a Higher Dimension.

Some Crystal Children appear to be developmentally delayed in their speech and do not talk until three or four years old. They are being labeled autistic. It is Virtue's contention that they communicate very well nonverbally and do not display the usual symptoms of autism such as poor eye contact, disconnection from other people and living lost in their own world. It is her belief that Crystal children have such advanced telepathic abilities they do not need to speak at an early age.[2-15] As responsible and caring adults, let us promote, instead of suppress, these extrasensory perceptions.

Create trust with Indigo and Crystal children by being present and sincere. As they grow to trust you and feel safe around you, they will open up and share what's real for them. Communication is a key for these wondrous children. Give them a voice, one child at a time. Ask them questions to find out where they are coming from and to understand their point of view. "What was that like for you?" "Then what happened?" "Tell me more." Draw out their beingness with open-ended phrases, "You feel sad because _____."

Give them a framework with the bigger picture. Let them know ahead of time what is going to happen. Also let them know when you absolutely need them to cooperate. "It's important to me that you cooperate while we are at _____." "I need you to cooperate during _____."

What will the world be like for today's children if we don't listen, nurture and teach them properly? What other means will they use to get their message across? If they indeed chose their parents, be grateful that it is you. We can happily choose to do our best, honoring and guiding these emissaries of truth.

While Nature versus Nurture has been the subject of debate for a long time, it does not really matter as much as you may think. Your uniquely wonderful child, no matter what wiring they were born with, will benefit greatly from a loving environment where you are there to assist in managing stress in healthy ways. And if you find that there are some things in your child's past that you regret (what parent doesn't?), know that everyone has the potential to relearn new patterns of behavior and neural processing. Brain plasticity and neuronal regeneration mean that we and our children retain the possibility to change for the better.

Genes alone will not determine how a child will succeed in school academically, socially and emotionally. Based on the research, there is no doubt that the quality of early childhood experience does shape a child's brain development in critical ways. Nature and nurture are both definitely important influences. The fact remains that parents can do nothing about the genes of their children short of the Human Genome Project, but they have a significant influence on the kind of environment they can provide. Parents can play their immense role with the "nurture" aspect and affect development and lifetime success.

Let nature take its course with nurture leading the way.

Brain inhibitors to
learning

"Stress interferes with a child's brain functions and processing for learning."

— Denise C. Hornbeak

Stress Inhibits Learning

What does it mean to you to be Stressed? Frustrated? Worried? Nervous? Fearful? In what ways do you notice it in your body? Where do you feel it in your body? How does it affect your breathing? What muscles become tense? What thoughts do you repeat over and over?

Stress allows for quick reactions to danger, but decreases the nervous system's ability to learn, remember or create. Stress inhibits learning. Under stress, activity in the mind and in the body is centered in the sympathetic nervous system, which prepares the body for a fight-or-flight reaction. As a result, brain activity in the limbic system, which first processes new information, and in the neo-cortex of the cerebrum, where abstract thinking and reasoning take place, are minimized. Only through movement that integrates visual, auditory and motor patterns can a child return to a stress-free state of learning.

The Stress Factor in the Early Years

The experience of stress is a critical factor during the early years as the brain is developing. Stress impedes the development of the child from conception. Every thought and action by the mother gives rise to biochemical changes for the fetus. Feelings of love, peace, harmony, security and joy create an extremely different chemical environment than stress hormones flooding the surrounding areas of the embryo and fetus caused by mother's emotions of fear, anxiety and anger.[3-1] If the fetus is in constant stress, seeds are sown for poor future stress tolerance and a predisposition for hypertension. Pregnant mothers have a significant choice in developing a positive influence for their growing baby.

Today's children are experiencing more stress than ever as the pressure from society and a constant stream of information requires keeping up with the Joneses, becoming screen-savvy with electronic media, looking and dressing according to style, and an insistence they excel academically and athletically amongst their peers. Information clutters our mind not only as adults but also as children. Many children are kept on such busy schedules that they are not connecting from the inside out.

When we are under stress, the body naturally releases the stress hormones adrenaline and cortisol. Adrenalin prepares the body to fight or flee when danger arises. Cortisol causes the breakdown of body tissues to supply enough energy to the muscles so you can fight or flee. The production of both are stimulated by adreno-cortico-tropic hormones.[3-2] Five minutes of anger keeps an excess of cortisol in the body for six hours. We want to destress to regain the innate interest and motivation to live, work and create, not to mention its benefits for the heart and whole body.

When a parent brings a child in for a consultation, I ask about the amount of time they spend sitting at the computer, watching television and the extent of their other electronic activity in a typical day. I usually recommend parents limit the time for electronics. Television, computer time and electronic games become stressful to the physiology of the body. They are also difficult to stop playing once the child has begun. Children need our guidance to limit the time. Today's kids know instinctively that it detrimentally affects them when played in excess. My son candidly told me after taking a break for two days from one of his hand-held games. "It's good that I haven't been doing Game Boy these days. I overreact a lot if I do too much electronics. It takes me longer to figure out numbers in math."

Our body chemistry and our perception of the task at hand determine how we respond. So if we arrive at work "stressed out" from some interaction at home or the demands of everyday life, we will automatically begin the day on edge because the body is actually in a state of overwhelm. How many of us rush for several cups of coffee just to jump start our day after a night's sleep?

Sources of Stress

Stress interferes with a child's brain functions and processing for learning. Stress from a variety of sources will inhibit learning. Among these are developmental, nutritional, medical, electrical, emotional, competitive, educational, environmental and electronic media.

1. Developmental – added stress can cause developmental delays as the physiology is focused on survival, thus there are incomplete neurological connections in the brain formation. Primary Learning Tools (PLTs) can enhance developmental growth.

2. Nutritional – we all have our out-of-control-kids sugar stories. It is an accepted fact that too much sugar affects behavior. When the body is given large amounts of sugar and carbohydrates and not enough water, essential fatty acids, amino acids and protein, it negatively affects brain function and overall health.

3. Medical – medical problems tax the nervous system. Health issues and physical/mental disabilities make the system work harder and use more energy to perform tasks. Because of the ears' link to the vestibular system and their effect on hearing human speech, ear infections in the early years also impair learning ease.

4. Electrical – EMFs (electromagnetic fields), particularly from fluorescent lights, cell phones, refrigerators and microwaves challenge the physiology. Electromagnetic fields, similar to those found in overhead power lines, can have a biological effect on living systems.

5. Emotional – main circumstances that trigger emotional stress
  • Emotional abuse by parents
  • Shouting by parents and teachers

Stress

"In my 35 years as a reading specialist, I have noticed that reading aloud for some students is the most stressful task, which affects their reading ability, enjoyment and learning progress."
– Isabel Cohen

- Divorce, death or illness in the family
- Reading aloud in front of the class and teacher (for some children)
- Fighting with family and friends
- Moving to a new home environment involving new friends and a new school

6. Competition – test taking, sibling rivalry, peer pressure and parental pressure to succeed in school, with musical instruments and in sports. Have you heard what some of the parents are yelling from the sidelines of a sporting event? Where is that aggression coming from? Let us be reminded that it is just a game and is meant to be fun and invigorating for children.

7. Rigid Educational Systems – the current public school system insists that children sit still, follow directions and compete for grades by conforming to teacher expectations. We are realizing that children are being expected to perform tasks that are developmentally inappropriate, such as reading and printing before the age of seven, when the body can more easily learn these skills. Today's rigid educational systems do not provide enough movement and in most states the funding cuts are eliminating important classes such as art, music and physical education from their curriculum.

8. Environmental Toxins – sounds, light, mold, mildew, heavy metals and chemical toxins affect learning. Some chemical cleaners, petroleum products and pesticides are so toxic they impair brain function. Effects can manifest in unexpected ways, such as a child's writing ability.

9. Vaccines – thimerosal, a preservative added to some vaccines, poses grave concern because it metabolizes to 49.5 percent ethyl mercury and thiosalicylate in the human body. It is especially toxic to a rapidly developing infant brain. Thimerosal has been linked to autism. It was introduced in the 1930s a few years before Leo Kanner, M.D., "discovered" a new mental disorder among children called autism. "Early on, autism was usually diagnosed in more affluent families. But as the vaccine became available to the masses, the diagnosis grew to include children from every socioeconomic level. In the 1980s and 90s as the HepB and Hib vaccines were added to the vaccine schedule, three times before six months of age, the diagnosis of autism skyrocketed.

In 2000, the American Academy of Pediatrics published a report to physicians on thimerosal in vaccines. The AAP, Public Health Service, and the CDC (Center for Disease Control) agreed that the use of thimerosal-containing vaccines should be reduced or eliminated due to potential risk. Unfortunately, despite this report and its recommendations, many pediatricians continue to administer thimerosal-laden vaccines due to the cost-advantages of being able to purchase and keep large quantities in storage. Pediatricians who have offices out of large hospitals are especially susceptible to this problem because they get their vaccines from the hospital, not an interdependent pharmaceutical company."[3-3]

10. **Electronic Media** – television, computers, iPods and video games - Have you noticed how kids get locked into these activities? The eyes lock into a stare and the body locks into a terror state and sensory overload.

This last source, electronic media, is the biggest concern for many families. Television, computer technology and global communication networks have connected the 6.7 billion people around the world and the effects actually manifest in the nucleus of the family. The technological explosion has affected how parents raise their children. Electronic equipment is being used as a distracting tool. When children, by their behavior are communicating their need to emotionally connect, the parent or childcare provider is distracting that primary need by turning on the television or computer.[3-4]

Television, computers and video games frequently replace other more interactive and meaningful activities, such as arts and crafts, reading, playing with friends, and other gross motor body movements in a child's daily life. They foster a sedentary life-style with a lack of exercise and whole-body movement.[3-5] Children need plentiful, positive interaction with other children and adults. Excessive TV viewing can negatively affect early brain development, the physical body and behavior. This is especially true at younger ages, when learning to talk and play with others is a child's main job. A 2004 study on the effects of early television exposure on subsequent attentional problems confirmed that early television watching at ages one and three is associated with decreased attention span at age seven. Researchers found that ten percent (10%) of the 2,623 subjects at age seven had attention problems correlating to the amount of hours viewed per day.[3-6]

Until more research is completed on the effects of TV on very young children, the American Academy of Pediatrics (AAP) recommends that children under two years of age not watch any television. For older children, the Academy recommends two hours or less per day of educational, nonviolent programs.[3-7] Following the recommendations of the AAP by limiting your child's screen time with the television, video games, hand-held electronics and computers to no more than one or two hours per day will tremendously improve the overall quality of their life.

According to the Nielsen Media Research, the total average time a household watched television during the 2005-2006 season was 8 hours and 14 minutes per day, a record high. The average amount of television watched by an individual viewer was 4 hours and 35 minutes, also a record.[3-8] The average home in a 2006 study had 4 television sets; nearly two-thirds had a television in the child's bedroom, and nearly half had a television set in the kitchen or dining room.[3-9] These statistics are astounding!

Viewing television extensively places a visual stress on the eyes. It bombards children with a constantly shifting stream of images and flickering that is too fast for the child to process. This over-stimulation leads to visual exhaustion, which causes ocular lock (staring) and auditory disassociation. If an adult walks in the room and sees a child glued to the television and not responding to their communication, that is their cue to have the child get up and move around, activating the eyes, ears and the rest of the body and returning the brain to a creative and active thinking state.

The eyes need to experience the world in 3-D to fully develop. Seeing a flat two-dimensional image of a red apple on television is very different than seeing, touching, smelling, tasting and hearing the crunch of a really juicy red apple. For the brain to learn shapes of forms and spatial awareness, the body must experience the whole.[3-10]

Watching television does affect how children learn. High-quality, nonviolent children's shows can have a positive effect on learning. Studies show that preschool children who watch educational TV programs do better on reading and math tests than children who do not watch those programs. When used carefully and deliberately, television can be a positive tool to help a child learn.[3-11] Some television shows teach positive social behaviors like sharing, cooperating and good manners. Conversely, many shows have a negative effect on children and adolescents. These innocent individuals are particularly vulnerable to the messages conveyed through the media to influence their perceptions and behaviors. Many young children are incapable of discriminating between what they see and what is real. Research has shown that the primary negative health effects manifest as violent and aggressive behavior, premature sexuality, poor academic performance, a decrease in body concept and self-image, poor nutrition, and a higher incidence of obesity and substance use and abuse. Research further reveals that even television news can traumatize children or lead to nightmares. In a random survey of parents with children in kindergarten through sixth grade, thirty-seven percent (37%) reported that their child had been frightened or upset by a television story in the preceding year.[3-12] High-quality television programs can have benefits for older children. However, for younger children, this is not the case. Use television with caution!

Using Movement as a Destressor!

In August of 2003, I offered an In-service on the Brain Gym program for the teachers in the Cardiff school district. It is very heart warming to observe teachers experience the benefits of the Brain Gym activities for themselves and become enthused to implement this movement-based program immediately in their classroom. Most teachers initially study Educational Kinesiology with its 26 Brain Gym movements because they have heard that it can enhance their students' learning ability and success in school. Within the first hour of the course, participants quickly discover that it can be used for themselves as a destressor, for focusing and organizational skills, and for other daily life activities.

▲ Hook-Ups part 1

For this particular group of Cardiff-by-the-Sea teachers, school was starting the following week. Jan, Kim and Danan, the teachers in the MAC class (MultiAge Classroom) took this opportune time to introduce some of the Brain Gym activities, in particular the PACE readiness routine, to the students during the first week of school.

One of the girls in the class was Elizabeth S., a friendly and delightful

▲ Hook-Ups part 2

child with Down syndrome, always ready with a beautiful smile. About a month after school started one of her teachers, Ms. Jan, excitedly told me that Elizabeth was benefiting from the Brain Gym movements she was doing in the classroom and she even did Hook-Ups at the dentist. Hook-Ups is a simple movement activity described as the tenth Tension Tamer on page 41.

This is how Elizabeth's mother, Joanne, relates the story:

"The first time I saw Elizabeth do Hook-Ups on her own was at her dentist appointment in September of 2003 when she was 7, Grade 2. I didn't know much about it yet. I just noticed that as she was sitting in the dentist's chair looking rather nervous, she did a Hook-Up. When I asked her why afterward, she told me it made her calm. The entire time that she was in the MAC class they did Hook-Ups routinely throughout the day."

I was so impressed with Elizabeth making the transference from school to the highly stressful situation of the dentist's office. She figured out for herself at the age of seven that if she did the Hook-Ups no matter where she was feeling nervous, it would make her "feel better" and "calm" her. Bless her dear heart!

On one of the first days of fourth grade, Elizabeth's teacher noticed her doing Hook-Ups as she waited in line so she had Elizabeth teach the class how to do it. Now the whole class does Hook-Ups when they are in line as well as other Brain Gym activities throughout the day.

Mother says:

"Over the past three or so years Elizabeth uses Hook-Ups all the time to calm herself. At her First Communion in May 2005 as she walked up the aisle she did Hook-Ups first. She has been involved in performances over the past three years with the MAC class and Christian Youth Theater. Although she loves being on stage I have seen her many times doing Hook-Ups while she is on stage. I have seen her do them at doctors' appointments and when she is in a crowd and may be feeling overwhelmed or 'stressed.' She also does them at school assemblies, when it is really loud. She just seems to do Hook-Ups automatically and without thinking when she is in a stressful situation."

Her mother's final words to me were,

"I think that it (Brain Gym) has truly made a difference in Elizabeth's life and I can't thank you enough."

The physiology of stress is strictly for survival in a life-threatening situation. We have applied it to non-survival situations and so our children mirror us and do the same. It is natural to feel some excitement and curiosity when faced with challenges and the unknown. From these changes, one has an opportunity to adapt, learn and grow. The problem arises when there is too much change or too many challenges all at once. This becomes overwhelming to the mind/body system, which applies the stress response, and for a young child it interrupts their developmental process.

It is important for parents to teach their children strategies for handling stress. Since children learn best by example, parents can model to their child how they deal with stress. They can show them a healthy response with relaxation activities such as deep breathing, taking a bubble bath, listening to music, meditation or having a massage. Another category of destressors is vigorous physical activity like sports, yoga and working out. By getting exercise, especially in the early morning, you will feel calmer and more focused throughout the day. Destress, and the innate interest and motivation to learn and to live are regained.

Stress allows for quick reactions to danger in order to survive, but in the process it produces incoherent wave patterns in the brain and in the heart, and decreases the child's ability to learn, remember or create. Sustained stress is detrimental to a child's development due to the physiological elements that induce changes in the psychological balance. Following are the top ten Tension Tamer Activities (PLTs). These destressors are particularly beneficial for the mother-to-be to incorporate during pregnancy to keep her stress level at a minimum.

Top 10 Tension Tamers

1. Sip plenty of water throughout the day
2. Smile Breathing
3. Giraffe
4. Vigorous Exercise
5. Nurturing Hands
6. Play the Aloha-ha-ha game
7. Personal Power Pose
8. Back Roller
9. Gorilla Thump
10. Hook-Ups

1. Sip plenty of water throughout the day as you send thoughts of relaxation into the water – The brain is composed of at least 90% water and the body is either 75% water (men) or 55% (women). Dehydration causes irritability, fuzzy short-term memory, slows metabolism, decreases the ability to focus on the computer or while reading, unclear thinking, and is the #1 trigger of daytime fatigue.[3-13, 3-14] A study by the National Institute for Diabetes and Digestive Disorders in Bethesda, Maryland showed people who began drinking enough water increased the oxygen carried to their brain by as much as 100 to 1,000 times.[3-15] What a simple solution to so many conditions.

Water

The general rule of thumb:

- Drink one ounce of water for every 3 pounds of body weight per day.

- Double the amount of water under stress.

- Sip a couple cups of water for each cup of a dehydrating liquid such as coffee, tea, alcohol or soda.

> "Our bodily systems are electrical. Ultimately, it is the electrical transmission within the nervous system that makes us sensing, learning, thinking, acting organisms. Water, the universal solvent, is essential for these electrical transmissions and for maintaining the electrical potential within our bodies."
>
> – Carla Hannaford [3-16]

A.W.'s grandmother relates the following about her 2½-year-old grandson who displays autistic behaviors. "His school couldn't believe when I picked him up how he would run to me asking for water, so they started having a water bottle available, too. They could see how much it helped calm him. Now, he always has his water bottle and he carries it around the house, asks for water, has it in the car."

2. Smile Breathing – Pause a moment. As you smile, inhale through the nose with your tongue on the roof of the mouth. Feel your body totally relax as you exhale through the nose. Mouth breathing tends to make people overbreathe and make nasal breathing more difficult. Reduce your breaths during this time to four per minute. This will require taking deeper and fuller diaphragmatic breaths, filling the lower lungs first like filling a glass of water from the bottom up. If your child is in a hyperventilated state with too much oxygen in the body, then choose to hold the breath out at the end of an exhale, before starting the cycle.

Variation: Pucker Breathing – Make your lips pucker instead of smile as you inhale. Take note of how you feel when you do it each way. What bodily responses do you notice? Is your vision affected? How's the rhythm of your breathing now?

3. Giraffe – Sit up straight, close your eyes and drop your shoulders. Now lengthen the neck muscles first by extending the head up and then dropping the head over to one side leading with the ear down to the shoulder. Deep breathe through the nose while feeling the neck muscles relaxing. Then raise the head back up to center, lowering the shoulders still further and lifting the head higher while noticing the difference between the two sides of the neck. Next drop the head to the other shoulder and repeat as before. Finally return your head to center, open your eyes and lift your head still higher while you imagine you're a giraffe surveying the African terrain. Enjoy your relaxed body and your colorful surroundings. Now guide your child through this Tension Tamer.

4. Vigorous Exercise – Brisk walking, cycling, swimming, and yoga or your favorite sport activity or hobby, e.g. singing and dancing have a destressing effect on the mind and body.

> "I truly believe that one of the best ways to release physical stress is through movement, sometimes slow and gradual, sometimes more aerobic or rhythmic. Different methods work better for different people. I have chosen yoga as a primary method because it seems to be accessible and attainable for almost everyone. The other benefit is that it can be helpful in resolving emotional or psychological stress as well as physical."
>
> — Chris Zeitler, Yoga Instructor

5. Nurturing Hands – While your child is sitting or lying down on their back, place one hand over your child's forehead and one hand at the base of their skull. Hold quietly, breathing and creating the space for them to balance themselves. This can be a very nurturing experience for them. Teach them that they can also do it themselves. It will calm "butterflies" in the stomach and balance the brain.

Variation: Add having them look up, with head leveled and eyes closed, while describing what they imagine up in the sky. One only need hold the slight gaze upward for a few seconds to gain the benefits of accessing an alpha state and dissolving fearful thoughts.

6. Play the Aloha-ha-ha game – Either in front of a mirror or with two or more people facing each other, take turns or simultaneously say Aloha-ha-ha. Emphasize the Ha-Ha-Ha. Feel the game transform into moments of ridiculous pleasure. Enjoy the laughter and sense of well-being while releasing more "feel good" dopamine, just like when you watch a funny movie.

7. Personal Power Pose – With closed eyes, deep breathe while holding Personal Power points or hold knees for one minute. The Personal Power points are just above the waistline on the back of the body at the adrenals. They are sometimes referred to as Pregnancy Pose points. Hold the hands behind the back with pinky fingers and ring fingers closest to the spine. Imagine the breath moving up the spine as you inhale.[3-17] This pose can revive exhausted adrenals and is refreshingly soothing.

8. Back Roller – Starting with a long cotton sock, put an old tennis ball inside, tie a knot, add a second tennis ball and tie a second knot.
Some adults prefer to use a wooden back roller because it provides deeper pressure. Lie down and place the roller under 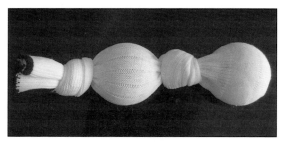 your back, down by the tailbone, with the balls straddling the spine and the soft knot under the spine. Passively rest and breathe deeply, then wiggle your back down the roller slowly, stopping along the way, so each section of the sides of the spine has a chance to release any tight muscles. Breathe into any pain you may experience from tension in your back. Breathing deeply also elongates the spine, facilitating greater blood and nerve flow throughout the body.

The Back Roller activity lengthens many muscles, stimulates circulation and rolls tension right off the back, directly affecting associating nerves, muscles and organs. The main set of muscles affected are the erector spinae, which run from iliac crest up to the occiput – covering the whole length of the spine from the tail to the head. Near the iliac and sacrum in the hip area you are accessing the quadratus lumborum muscle and moving up the back, the latissimus dorsi, the trapezius and rhomboids. All acupressure points stimulated along the spine serve to improve circulation, relax the nervous system, balance the respiratory system, balance all internal organs and relax the spine. An added bonus – stimulating the transverse processes (and a bit of the spinous) signals the body to release endorphins.[3-18]

By doing it themselves, children will not only experience all the benefits listed above, but will be able to control the amount of deep pressure, improve their body awareness and reap the rewards of independently choosing a way to feel better.

9. Gorilla Thump – Thump your upper chest like a gorilla 2" below the notch at the collar bone and add those Gorilla sounds. Gorillas naturally thump their chest when they are scared, anxious or feel threatened in some way to give them courage and enliven their body. Stress disturbs our polarity. The Gorilla thump corrects this reversal and also corrects the spin of all chakras.[3-19] It also activates the thymus of the immune system.

10. Hook-Ups – Extend the arms out in the front of the body with thumbs up and then thumbs down, cross the arms, intertwine the fingers of each hand and pull them up to rest on the chest. Cross the legs at the ankles. Place the tongue on the roof of the mouth as you inhale and feel the body relax as you exhale. Relax in this position until you feel a sense of restful alertness throughout your body. Then uncross the hands and legs and connect the fingertips of each hand together – thumb-to-thumb, pointer-to-pointer, etc.[3-20] The palms are not touching. The hands will appear like a lotus blossom. The Hook-Ups calm the central nervous system and restore our polarity by correcting the flow of energy of the body.

Now take a move-*meant* to reconnect with your inner peace center.

Lack of movement

Movement is a key ingredient in the entire process of brain and early childhood development. As explained by Dr. Jean Ayres, movement aids the brain in organizing sensations. Sensory stimulation will lead to adaptive responses, which in turn will lead to sensory integration. For example, a girl on a bicycle will make adaptive responses after sensing the pull of gravity and the movement of her body when she feels herself losing balance. The adaptive response in this case is shifting the weight of the body to prevent her from falling off the bicycle. The child makes the adjustment and continues the ride. Another adaptive response is with the steering. The girl will make adjustments with the handles after sensing the visual stimuli so she can direct the bike where she wants to go. After the girl finishes a bike ride, she has integrated many sensations. Her brain has learned more about gravity, the space around her, and how her body moves. With this new neurological wiring, riding will be easier the next time.[3-21]

Are we depriving our children of opportunities to develop?

What is happening to the development of a baby who is in a car seat while the mother drives the car to do errands, is kept in the car seat in all of the stores since it expediently fits on the cart, and left for another few hours in the car seat because the infant fell asleep from the motion of the car on the way home? Today's all-in-one car seat/stroller is very convenient for parents, but deprives a child of the necessary movement they need for brain development. The baby is confined in a rigid 45° angle and inhibited from active movement of the neck and core muscles.[3-22] In addition, playpens cause toddlers to be unnecessarily restrained. Jump seats and walkers position babies vertically, which prompts the premature development of some muscle groups while limiting others.[3-23]

Contrary to common parental beliefs, infant walkers when used extensively may impair instead of foster an infant's motor and mental development. According to Dr. A. Carol Siegel,

> **Infant Walkers**
>
> Contrary to common parental beliefs, infant walkers when used extensively may impair instead of foster an infant's motor and mental development.
>
> – Dr. A. Carol Siegel

experimental psychologist at Case Western Reserve University in Cleveland, Ohio and Dr. Roger V. Burton, developmental psychologist at the State University of New York at Buffalo, walking and other gross milestones are delayed when babies use walkers for about 2½ hours per day. Siegel and Burton studied 109 infants between the ages of six and fifteen months. The data concluded that infants who used walkers sat, crawled and walked later than the nonusers. They scored lower on the Bayley scales of mental and motor skills than the nonwalker group. Walkers interfere with the natural process of locomotor skills, block the critical role of visual feedback in developing motor systems and have an adverse effect on overall mental development.[3-24] If you must use a walker, use it with caution for a limited period, and not as an entertainment tool.

> ## Crawling
>
> Crawling gets both sides of the body working together, including the eyes for binocular vision, the ears for binaural hearing, and the arms and legs.

Infant walkers, playpens, jump seats and car seats all inhibit natural developmental movement to some degree. Their utilization replaces some of the vitally important time essential for crawling and other activities on the stomach. Research indicates that children who miss the full experience of the crawling stage later exhibit learning challenges, especially with reading. The cross-lateral movement of crawling activates development of the nerve pathways between the two hemispheres of the neocortex, called the corpus callosum. Crawling gets both sides of the body working together, including the eyes for binocular vision, the ears for binaural hearing, and the arms and legs. The senses will be more fully accessible with this equal stimulation and the whole body will move in a more integrated and efficient fashion.[3-25]

As previously discussed, parental influence begins during the gestation period. Pregnant mothers can use stress-management methods to keep their stress levels low and the embryo and fetus in a biochemically safe surrounding for proper development. Speaking in "parentese" and reading to the fetus, especially rhyming books like Dr. Seuss, during the last six weeks of pregnancy are beneficial auditory experiences. Prenatal factors to avoid are both recreational and some pharmaceutical drugs like antibiotics, environmental toxins and alcohol.

Stress factors play a key role in inhibiting development and learning. Research studies, especially since the well-known Spitz series and the Prescott and Harlow studies, prove that sensory stimulation is mandatory for newborn infants. Moreover, it is critical that they move because a baby's brain needs exercising for their budding motor pathways. The brain is a chain of communicating cells. Every touch, emotion and movement is translated into chemical and electrical activity that modifies the way a child's brain is wired together. The following chapters will be filled with learning tools to support the need for movement throughout the growing years.

You've got to move it, move it, move it.

Reflexes as foundational

> **"It is the development of normal Infant Reflexes and their integration into the general system of body movements . . . which leads to fullest formation of body dimensions and related brain functions."**
>
> — Svetlana Masgutova

Most people are familiar with the knee-jerk reaction that instantly occurs when the doctor taps on the tendon just below your kneecap with a small rubber mallet, but there are numerous other reflexes. Collectively they form a blueprint for every stage of brain-body development. There are primitive reflexes, lifelong reflexes, postural reflexes, birthing reflexes, facial reflexes, etc. In this chapter we will primarily discuss the primitive reflexes and how they are developmentally supportive of the subsequent stages of growth.

Any reflex is a primary movement given by nature. It is a response to internal or external stimuli which has protective or survival meaning and serves for development. An infant would not survive without the reflexive response to root, suck and swallow for nourishment. These are the precursors to the skill of chewing to keep the body alive and nourished. All skills start reflexive and all reflexes together form our skills.

Reflexes and movement patterns are essential parts of the developmental stages of the central nervous system. The reflexive responses stimulate the nervous system to grow. Reflexes shape and strengthen the patterns of motor development. The successful integration of the primitive reflexes into a baby's body allows for the emergence of the postural reflexes that are imperative in the development of motor patterns, balance, speech, vision and hearing. Motor development is the specific process by which a baby develops the system of neural pathways that takes in information through the senses, organizes and interprets that information, and then responds to it. Thus all information coming into a child's awareness is processed through an elaborate system of nerve networks in the brain and body. This system continues developing throughout life. The motor actions of touching and moving add meaning to the senses of vision and hearing. As these develop together, they form the complete network of information-processing pathways.

Primitive Reflexes

Primitive reflexes are the building neuro-patterns for the development of our vestibular, ocular, auditory, tactile and kinesthetic motor systems, and form the basis of our movement-based behaviors in life. They are automatic, involuntary, physical responses directed from the brain stem and have been developing since conception. These reflexes function without any involvement from the thinking centers of the right and left hemispheres of the neocortex.[4-1] In utero, reflex movement opens up the links between the different parts of the hindbrain, thus becoming the interlink mechanism of the back brain system.[4-2]

> **Reflexes**
>
> Without the freedom to move and have physical activity, a child does not integrate the primitive reflexes.

Much of brain development is based on early primitive reflex patterns that facilitate the growth and advancement of the brain. These reflex patterns are designed for survival in utero, and as newborns and infants. The maturation of the primitive reflexes is dependent on specific developmental movement patterns. Without the freedom to move and have physical activity, a child does not integrate the primitive reflexes.

Later on when there is distress, these unintegrated reflexes, may become active again, which keeps a person in survival mode, and inhibits the ability to participate, interact, process and communicate. Brain Gym® works specifically with these developmental movement patterns to rewire and re-set the brain/body system, and is based strongly on the theory of innate intelligence, i.e., the body knows exactly what it needs.

Reflexes in the Delivery Room

Instantaneously after birth, newborns depend on this set of primitive reflex responses. The reflexes are necessary for survival and adaptation outside the womb. For example, the rooting reflex drives the infant to find the nipple within minutes of birth. Once the nipple is located with the highly sensitive mouth, the sucking reflex will make it possible to decrease the high levels of adrenaline and cortisol that were needed for the birth process, and the sucking allows the newborn to take nourishment from mother's milk. These two reflexes are the baby's first internal experiences that translate into feeling satisfaction, contentment and security.[4-3]

Some babies develop while in utero a neuro-developmental predisposition for dyslexia, hyperlexia (above-average ability to read accompanied with a below-average ability to understand the spoken language), autism, etc. In some of these cases, the mothers during pregnancy experienced emotional traumas which were transferred to their child. As a result, some of the reflexes that usually develop when a baby is in utero do not develop correctly, causing incomplete neurological connections in the brain formation.

A baby goes through many developmental stages from conception. The primitive reflexes, such as the Fear Paralysis reflex, Moro reflex, Asymmetrical Tonic Neck reflex, Spinal Pereze reflex, Babinsky reflex, Robinson Grasp reflex, Spinal Galant reflex and Symmetrical Tonic Neck reflex, must emerge, be activated and then become fully integrated into the body system in order for children to continue to grow and to develop at their optimum. Reflexes are the springboards for the emergence of the developmental movement patterns and the movement patterns facilitate the reflexes transforming to their integrated state.

For example, the Asymmetrical Tonic Neck reflex (ATNR) is an automatic response of the limbs when the head is turned either spontaneously by the infant or passively by another person. For the period between thirteen weeks in utero until about six months of age, each time the head turns, the arm and leg on that side of the body extends and the opposite limbs flex. The development of this reflex in utero supports kicking activity, muscle tone and vestibular stimulation. Sometimes pregnant

---

mothers will feel a kick when the leg extends in the womb, especially during the last trimester.

The ATNR is a critical part of the birthing process along with the Spinal Pereze reflex, Symmetrical Tonic Neck reflex, Babinsky reflex, Head Righting reflex, Spinal Galant reflex and Crawling reflex with the latter serving to move the fetus into position and/or for coming out of the birth channel. The ATNR is a transitional reflex between each of the four stages of birth. The baby spontaneously turns its head with an ATNR response, stops for a pausing moment to slow down the birthing motion and protect against excessive neck rotation. These transitional periods will become the future pausing moments of integration in the learning process after a period of learning something new. A SuperConfitelligent young child will naturally play and be able to learn amidst the play, and also stop and relax to process the new information.

Nuchal cord

• The umbilical cord wrapped around the neck, limiting delivery of baby.

After birth, mother's familiar voice greeting her newborn will trigger baby to crawl up mother's stomach, skin to skin, to her chest, suck for nourishment and bond. Oxytocin is the hormone that not only stimulates uterine contraction during childbirth and milk ejection during lactation, but also creates the bond between mother and baby. A newborn looks into mother's eyes and mother just wants to return the gaze for hours. Oxytocin is our natural bonding chemical. Mother receives the hormonal message that everything is fine when baby crawls on her skin to her breasts and makes eye contact. In this way the postpartum symptoms of depression in many cases can be avoided. The brain of mother and newborn register that the birth has occurred and they are both safe, whole and bonded to each other for life. Taking the time to bond on mother's stomach activates the bonding reflex.

Hypotonic

• Having less than normal tone or tension, as of muscles or arteries.

In hospitals today, doctors are increasing the opportunity for bonding of mother and newborn as early as medically possible, given the various situations that can arise. Expectant mothers can request the umbilical cord remain connected during this bonding period and only be cut after it stops pulsating. At this point mother's blood is no longer mixed with the newborn's and baby is getting oxygen from the atmosphere. Fathers may be able to cut the umbilical cord if the baby is doing fine and having no complications. Yet, this is not feasible if the baby has a tight nuchal cord, if the baby is hypotonic or showing signs of distress, or if the couple decides to bank the baby's cord blood. Cord blood banking is becoming increasingly performed due to the potential for regenerative medical applications.[4-4]

In general, a vaginal birth is the better choice since so many reflexes are triggered during the delivery and the bonding can occur before the umbilical cord is cut. Yet, for those having an at-risk C-Section, there is still the opportunity to consciously activate baby's Bonding reflex. Although it is not feasible to breast-feed during the operation, the newborn may be placed next to mother's head and neck, assuming they are fine and don't need neonatal intensive critical care. The newborn sees mother smiling and hears her voice, "You are so wanted." "We are so happy you are here." Once the C-Section is completed and after they are wheeled off together to the post-partum room, baby is next placed on mother's abdomen or chest to feel her embrace and breast-feed. With baby on mother's chest there is also a completion of the third phase of the Moro reflex, which teaches us to share our fears and our need for protection by hugging another person. With this bonding process, best experienced in the first hour after birth, a strong foundation of trust and feelings of safety and security formulate so baby can adapt to this new world and relate for a lifetime in a healthy emotional and physical way.[4-5]

Newborn steps

- Newborn sees mother's smile
- Hears her voice of acceptance
- Crawls to nipple
- Begins sucking
- Calms down after intense experience of birth
- Feels nourished
- Bonds with mother for healthy attachment
- Feels the contentment of getting what they need

Touching the tongue of a newborn awakens the sucking reflex, which in turn stimulates the vestibular nerves and the cranial bones. When the nipple or other object, like the thumb or fingers, reaches the boundary of the hard and soft palate, the basic movement pattern of deep sucking occurs. This area between the hard and soft palate stimulates the sphenoid bone, and other cranial and facial bones of the skull connected to it, thus moving the cranial bones. Sucking brings rhythm to the sphenoid bone and the whole body. Rhythm is key in learning to read, succeed with academics and excel at sports.

Infants naturally deep suck 6-8 times, breathing easily and then swallowing. Deep sucking gives pleasure, inner peace and activates the sphenoid bone to release endorphins and calm the baby. The tongue will physically go into a spoon shape position in order to deep suck. By contrast with most bottled nipples, the tongue stays only behind the front teeth. The sucking is not strong and milk gathers in the back of the mouth. When the Rooting and Sucking reflexes are not fully integrated, the following effects may manifest: poor articulation, extended thumb sucking, chewing and biting pencils and fingernails, and a difficulty forming peer relationships.

All In Good Time

So what is happening to all our children who are not getting a natural birthing experience because their parents are opting for a scheduled C-Section or a baby is delivered breech? What neurological and sensory integrating problems will they face as a result? Of course if it's a life-threatening situation, a C-Section will be ordered, but what about the families that plan the birth date like scheduling a vacation instead of letting nature take its course? A baby's birth is the biggest and strongest learning experience of their life. Nature designed it for the baby to start the birth process by releasing hormones into the blood stream to tell the expectant mother, "I'm ready." "I'm ready to leave this dark, wet womb and enter a new world."

Making the delivery at nature's time is ideal for the infant's growth, development and completion of the gestation period, and it is the last pregnancy phase for the mother. It will affect how the infant will learn, how they approach new challenges, how they organize their thoughts, feelings and world, how they are with transitions and whether or not completing projects come naturally for them.

As infants, it is again important that we allow babies to do what they do naturally, without artificial support. A baby must thoroughly experience life on their stomach and back, and then their hands and knees before standing upright. Rolling over is connected with controlling the movement of lifting the head and then the upper part of the trunk. The ability to lift the head gives a new perspective of the world to the infant.[4-6] Exploring the world from these vantage points is crucial for a child before becoming a walking human being. So even if your infant likes that bouncer or cradle swing to see the world, remember that working to lift the head, turn, and sit up are important developmental milestones that babies can and should learn on their own.

Unintegrated Reflexes and Learning Problems

The study of the primitive reflexes provides a plethora of symptoms resulting from unintegrated reflexes that directly affect learning and behavior, and cause school problems. For the Moro reflex, the list of possible long-term symptoms include hypersensitivity, a low tolerance to stress, allergies, a weak immune system, shyness, losing control, swearing and lashing out, chronically hypervigilant, easily distracted in the classroom, etc. This primitive reflex is triggered in response to sudden auditory, visual and tactile stimuli. It normally is fully integrated by 4-6 months after the expected date of delivery.

The Symmetrical Tonic Neck reflex, also referred to as the STNR, aids an infant in defying gravity by lifting the head to look forward. This reflex is the precursor to creeping, crawling, standing and walking. Children with a unintegrated STNR are frequently observed holding their head up with one hand when sitting at a desk reading or writing. They may have poor eye-hand coordination and difficulties with activities that require refocusing from near to far like writing information that has been written on the blackboard.[4-7]

Sixty percent (60%) of Americans have an STNR that is not integrated. If the neck is still in control of the body, when the head goes down, the legs go out when sitting. This looks like slouching or else the person will hook the ankles of the feet around the legs of a chair, or sit on one leg or their feet stay active, thumping and fidgeting, and they can't focus. They may appear very uncomfortable in their body and are sloppy eaters. As the head is raised the arms extend and food that was headed for the mouth lands on the table or floor.[4-8]

As children, we all went through developmental reflexes. For example, when babies are on their tummy, they will naturally want to lift their head (Neck reflex-STNR) ▶ automatically stretch out arms ▶ creep ▶ up on all fours (hands and knees) ▶ rock ▶ crawl. Crawling activates the two sides of the brain to work together, resulting in the integration of brain and body for optimal brain function and learning.

Reflexes are fundamental because they activate the brain for protection in order for development to occur. Developmentally, they are supportive of the next levels. Reflexes are resources given by nature and must first be awakened before addressing physical and mental skills. If reflexes are not activated or integrated, they will not support these skills. It becomes a readiness issue, which is the crux of preparing a child to succeed in school and ultimately in life. For instance, the Asymmetrical Tonic Neck reflex (ATNR) and the Grasp reflex are both foundational for writing. If a child starts writing with the ATNR still retained, you will see them straighten the writing arm each time they turn their head to that side. So Paul may be writing along and then look up to see what Johnny is doing at the desk next to him and, unexpectedly, his arm shoots out, making a big line on his (Paul's) paper. According to Dr. Svetlana Masgutova, a prominent neurokinesiologist, a unintegrated ATNR is one of the most prevalent reasons for school failure. Some of the long-term effects are lack of memory processes, reading and listening difficulties, poor language development and confused handedness, poor sense of direction and balance, handwriting problems, difficulties crossing the midline and focusing.[4-9]

There is a natural overlapping of the developmental stages through childhood. Each stage contains elements of multiple, previous stages. Because all the stages are so intertwined, any missing links can lead to problems in memory, organization, perception, creativity and sequencing as well as imbalances in the physical body systems and movement capabilities.

It's Your Turn

Take a break in reading now and lie down on your stomach. Roll over without using your hands or your legs. Where does the movement originate in your body? What parts of your body are moving the most? Now lie on your back with legs straight on the carpet or a pad on the floor. How can you move your buttocks to your feet again without using your hands or moving your feet? We might understand the world with our mind, but we really learn with our body. So get up and head to the floor to explore these questions with your body. Close your book to take an exploration break.

How was that? Our little ones must figure this out in those early months of life in order to move forward to the next stages.

Can Reflexes be Linked to Potty Training?

A mother came to me very concerned that her 3½-year-old daughter, Anastasia, would not be able to start preschool the following week. The school had a policy that no children were allowed to attend unless they were potty trained. We discussed how stressful any unfamiliar situation away from mother or the primary caregiver can be for a young girl or boy. Potty training itself can be very traumatic for both parents and children if the adults have specific expectations and must follow a schedule.

Children are much more intelligent than we realize — I cannot emphasize this point enough. They instinctively know what they require to bring their brain/body system back into balance and function properly. When appropriately facilitated, this intelligence can be drawn out and implemented. In this case Anastasia only needed to lengthen a specific calf muscle called the gastrocnemius. By having Anastasia lie down with legs straight, her mother was able to assist her in lengthening this calf muscle by pointing and flexing her feet one at a time.[4-10] The emphasis was on the dorsiflexion/calf-lengthening, which helped to relax the Tendon Guard reflex and balance the bladder meridian. An optional variation involves the adult placing a hand on the top of the child's foot or feet simultaneously with slight pressure so that the child responds by flexing the foot up towards the shin. We make a game of this by saying, "Bring your Toes to your Nose." The advantage of the first version is it can be done while the child is asleep. The advantage of the variation is two-fold: (1) the child participates more actively; (2) it becomes a fun game! It is my experience that children make shifts easier through play.

Did the bladder meridian get unblocked? Most definitely! The bladder meridian, one of the longest in the body, runs from the head down the back along both sides of the spine, all the way to the toes, passing through the calf muscles at some very potent points. And as is the nature of meridians, release in one area helps facilitate release along the whole length. Balancing this meridian not only benefits the bladder, it helps to release fear and stress, and can improve sleep as well.[4-11]

Did the gastrocnemius calf muscle get lengthened? Absolutely! Anyone who does the activity can feel the lengthening up the entire back side of the body. Did the Tendon Guard reflex get reset to its homeostasis of relaxed and ready? Yes, indeed! Was the Tendon Guard reflex released? That was our intention. The Tendon Guard reflex (TGR), a Lifelong reflex, becomes activated when a person is under stress or perceives danger. Problems develop with prolonged activation of this sympathetic response when there is no parasympathetic resting, releasing and balancing response. Sometimes the body stays in this survival state for years, affecting daily life activities and behaviors. Release of this Tendon Guard reflex promotes a parasympathetic response, allowing the child to return to a relaxed, focused state with conscious awareness of bodily sensations and better control of bodily functions.

Sometimes the three phases of the Moro reflex, the Spinal Pereze and/or the Spinal Galant reflexes have not matured and are still overly active or retained. Addressing these reflexes with a trained specialist integrates them and resolves the bedwetting or bladder control issues, which possibly originated with the stress hormone levels in utero.[4-12]

Learning Pyramids

Reflexes do not stand alone. Usually there is learning pyramid involvement when we see retained reflexes. Examining the stages of the learning process can provide us with the understanding of the learning tools that we, as parents, can use with our children. Several experts have created their Learning Pyramids to reflect a theoretical foundation and diagram for this developmental process. Each stage of child development builds on the one beneath it in the pyramid. As stated by Heiniger and Randolph, "The pyramid is a model of the developmental sequences of education. We marvel at our failure to realize what is so obvious – that learning is a total mind, body and spirit experience. Learning in any area, physical, emotional, intellectual, or spiritual, involves the whole person. Anyone in a helping profession must be cognizant of the interdependence of all areas and all professions."[4-13]

The motor skills of balance, dynamic balance, body awareness, locomotor skills, cross-laterality, laterality and bi-laterality play a supportive role at the foundation of all skill growth. Experts concur that when any of the motor skills have not been properly developed, there will be a significant impact on the child's learning ability for all subsequent skills and for succeeding in school.

W. Jean Foster, the developer of Motorobics, explains the learning process to be like a tower of blocks. If one of the blocks at the bottom is either smaller or missing, it will cause the whole tower to be unsteady and malfunction or completely collapse.[4-14] The degree of severity of the developmental delay is demonstrated when the child attempts reading, writing and math both at school and at home. Studying requires extraordinary effort with mental energy expended extensively for hours only to barely receive a passing grade.

The higher-level thinking processes of association, deduction, induction, analysis, synthesis, organization, sequencing and abstract thinking, and the cognitive areas of conceptualization, patterning, verbal ability, visual discrimination, perceptual speed, reasoning and memory necessitate motor skills functioning congruently, supported by a balanced autonomic system. When problematic developmental patterns are effectively addressed, the reflexes are naturally integrated. There are specialized licensed Brain Gym consultants/Educational Kinesiologists trained to draw out potential in specific cases.

Infant PLTs

The following are specific Primary Learning Tools to support an infant's development:

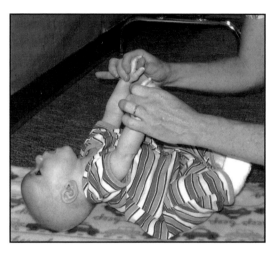

- **Birth to 3 months**
  – *Part one:* With baby on back, first press your thumbs in their tiny palms and watch for their mouth to open and the head to move forward or turn to the side (Babkin Palmomental reflex).
- **Birth to one year**
  – *Part two:* Now slide thumbs horizontal in hands so baby can grip them (Robinson Grasp reflex).[4-15] Then slowly and gently raise them up a few inches to strengthen the neck muscles.

- **Three months to one year** – Lay baby on stomach, place a toy or object in front of them to facilitate reaching with the head and/or hands and to encourage eye-hand coordination, hand-to-hand coordination and forward movement.

- **First year** – Lay baby on back or stomach and turn their head so the right ear is up. This position activates the right ear for sounds and creates the dominance for speech in the left hemisphere where Broca's and Wernicke's speech centers are located. Broca is the center for speech expression and articulation. Wernicke is the center for hearing human speech. Periodically resting baby in this position coordinates hearing and seeing.[4-16]

- **First year** – Lots of *Tummy Time*. With baby on their stomach, sit or stand in front of your baby's head and encourage them to lift their head and chest by singing or making unusual sounds or shaking a rattle. This will entice your infant to look and then lift up their torso. During *Tummy Time* your baby is learning to reach with their head. Breech-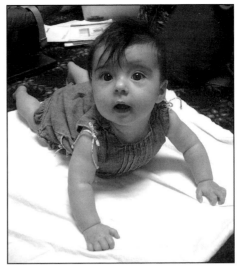
and Cesarean-birth babies require an ample amount of this activity since they didn't have this developmental experience during the birthing process. This undeveloped pattern is seen with many children exhibiting ADD/ADHD symptoms.[4-17]

- **First 2 years**– Alternate sides you hold baby when breast- or bottle-feeding. The head is slightly flexed with chin down for ease of swallowing. The outside hand, arm and leg will be free for kneading and kicking.

PLTs for Life

The following are Primary Learning Tools that can be used throughout life.

- **Birth to age 99** – *Passive Rolling of the Bottom:* Baby lies on tummy. While you hold on to the diaper or waistband of pants, rhythmically roll the bottom gently from side to side. With babies you will start noticing the hands and
arms moving and head lifting. The back and bottom may also

start to rise as a precursor to crawling. For older children and adults position the forehead on the hands. After a while they will be able to initiate the movement on their own. Most people experience this rhythmic movement as very calming, while also activating the cerebellum and cortex. [4-18]

- **Birth to age 99** – Play *Superman* with your child. Start on the floor on your tummy and arms extended to the sides flying with head, chest and legs lifted off the floor. Imagine flying above a city or countryside and tell stories of what you see down below. A precursor to *Superman* for newborns from day one is spending time on mother or father's chest, preferably skin to skin. After baby can hold their head up, arms can be extended and even the whole body lifted up from under the baby's armpits in flight.
  Variation: Baby lies on your legs or place the bottom of your feet on their chest while you hold their hands and lift your legs. (It's a great abdominal workout for you, too!)

- **Birth to age 99** – Softly brush or stroke the side of each foot from the heel to the baby toe to initiate the uncurling and fanning of the toes.[4-19]

- **Birth to age 99** – Blow a tiny puff of air in the face to elicit the Blink reflex. This causes a natural blink and breaks a stare.

- **Two to age 99** – Crawl around together playfully and then get up to your feet to run around and skip. Many children develop the ability to coordinate skipping about 4 years of age. They will start learning earlier, though, by watching and imitating you doing it.

- **Two to age 99** – Bounce on a mini trampoline with arms extended up and outward to elicit the Joy reflex. An adult can hold a child's hands up for support as they bounce.

- **Two to age 99** – Lie on your chest/hips on a scooter board or big pillow pretending to be an animal or a boat while moving forward with your hands.

- **Three to age 99** – Crazy Straw[4-20] Encourage your child to hold a crazy straw in the center of their mouth, close their eyes and drink the water slowly and rhythmically, relaxing between sips. Spreading the amount throughout the day,

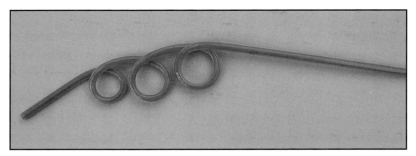

match your child's age to the number of ounces of water — a 4-year-old would sip 4 ounces per day. The more they suck, the stronger the sucking may become. Drinking through a crazy straw with lots of curls or twists provides more than hydration. It can benefit the following functions:

- **Inter-hemispheric integration** – By sucking through the straw held in the center of the mouth, the two sides of the mouth and cheeks integrate, thereby stimulating the two cerebral hemispheres in a coordinated rhythmic fashion. Inter-hemispheric integration is needed to be able to process language, balance logic with our instincts, and other functions frequently compromised in neurobehavioral disorders and in brain injury.

- **Binocular functions with the two eyes teaming together and eye contact** – By sucking, our trigeminal nerves are stimulated, and they in turn help regulate many aspects of our vision, including the ability of our eyes to converge, i.e. both eyes focusing together on a target.

- **Light sensitivity** – One reason that people become light sensitive is that the two eyes do not team in their processing of the visual images which, of course, is based on perception of light and darkness. Another reason is that the pupils have a reduced degree of reactivity to light. In other words, the muscles around the pupil are meant to contract in bright light to reduce the amount of light coming in the eyes. Drinking through the straw enhances these functions and thereby reduces light sensitivity.

- **Sound sensitivity and focused auditory attention–** Stimulation of the trigeminal and facial nerves directly affects functioning in the middle ear. We are all familiar with how chewing gum or sucking on hard candy helps people to tolerate the pressure change in their ears during take-off and landing on flights. And through a connection in the part of the midbrain called the colliculus, visual focus directs auditory focus.

- **Articulation** – Crazy straw sucking increases tongue and lip control and coordinated breathing, all of which support our ability to speak with clear, distinct articulation.

- **Non-verbal communication** – This ability is improved with facial muscle tone modulation.

- **Bowel and bladder control** – Paula Garbourg discovered that there is a relationship between all the sphincter muscles in our body. By strengthening any of our sphincter muscles (such as the lips and also the esophagus) we stimulate all the sphincters in our body, including the pupils of the eyes and the bowel and bladder.[4-21]

- **Hormonal Production** – Sucking also stimulates the pituitary gland for balance production of hormones, including the human growth factor hormone.

Precaution:

1. If the individual has a tendency for crossed-eyes, have them look at a distant object while drinking, rather than with closed eyes.
2. Do NOT use a crazy straw during pregnancy because the intense sucking may promote premature contractions.
3. Do NOT engage in intense sucking if you have glaucoma, retinal irregularities or a high risk of aspiration.
4. Rinse the straw after each use for sanitary purposes.

Reflexes are Foundational

An infant's first basic moves are inevitably reflexive in response to environmental stimuli. The side of the mouth is touched and the head automatically turns. The outer edge of the sole of the foot is stroked from heel to baby toe and the toes of the feet involuntarily spread. These primitive reflexes are the neurological basis for the developmental stages. They are fundamental in setting the stage for a baby's drive to roll over, sit, creep, push up to all fours and crawl, and later to find their way to standing upright and walking. Highly refined movement relies on a strong foundation of integrated reflexes and developmental movements.

This foundation of integrated reflexes is critical for a child to develop graceful, controlled movements in school, both at their desk reading and writing and out on the playground playing.

Movement is the link to
learning

"Movement activates the neural wiring throughout the body, making the whole body the instrument of learning."

— Carla Hannaford

One weekend in late winter, a group of sons and mothers from the Y Explorers had an event at Camp Marston, nestled in the mountains of Julian and surrounded by 230 acres of pine trees and hiking trails. Everyone was particularly excited because it had been snowing, and in Southern California that is a big deal for these city boys. They had their sleds, flying saucers and toboggans ready for some fast riding fun.

The Y Explorers is part of the Adventure programs at the YMCA. It is geared for moms and their young sons who want to spend quality, uninterrupted time together creating invaluable memories at special events like camping, swimming, paddle boating, rock climbing, BMXing and community service. The boys have a safe environment to do what they do best– play, laugh, explore and rough-and-tumble. There are also tribes for dads and daughters, too!

At this particular mother/son weekend event, five families were sharing a bunkhouse. The boys played non-stop in the snow all day until they were so soaked it was time to go in and dry out before dinner. Actually, they were drenched before lunch, but nobody cared; they were having too much fun.

One boy who attended was Ryder D., age 10, from Encinitas. Ryder has Cerebellar Hypoplasia, which means he was born with a nonfunctioning cerebellum. The cerebellum controls our muscular coordination for gross and fine motor skills, and is an essential part of producing normal, smooth, coordinated movement. It has a direct link to the neocortex. The cerebellum is key to maintaining our balance and sustaining our upright normal posture. Ryder's mother, Susan, describes it as "the subconscious body-movement decision-maker."

Imagine the impact a nonfunctioning cerebellum would have on a child with walking, chewing and speaking. Imagine his frustration level for communicating his needs. Ryder had severe ataxia, which is an extreme lack of coordination of the muscles of the body, affecting the control of body posture, motor coordination, speech and eye movements. He would typically stand with feet planted far apart, and sway while standing, struggling to maintain balance. He wore a helmet for many years to protect his head from all the falls. Neither could his hands respond quick enough to brake the fall before he got hurt. That protective reaction just wasn't there.

Susan was happy to find a group that sincerely welcomed them. She was determined to create experiences for Ryder so he could have "bits of success here and there." This trip was extra special for both of them.

On that Saturday, Ryder first played off to the side, away from all the boys who were sliding down the hill. He was building an igloo some of the time alone and some of the time with Gus, a 6-year-old boy.

Moving Moment

When the boys went back to the bunkhouse late Saturday afternoon, the bunk beds beckoned them. The urge to move is instinctive in children. They naturally started climbing and crawling from one bunk bed to another. With five bunk beds and four twin beds, seven boys expressed their exploratory spirits! And, best of all, Ryder was right in there with them playing "Follow the Leader" for about 30 minutes.

Susan and I took turns spotting Ryder on the sly to keep him safe. Quite honestly, he was able to do it all and keep up with them impressively. I knew this would have a profound effect on his muscular coordination and abilities and my reward was confirmed during the following day's outing.

On Sunday we all headed to the hills to slide. Ryder's mother assumed he was going to play with the igloo and watch the other boys sliding. She walked him over to the area where she felt he would be comfortable. All of a sudden, he appeared where all the mothers were, about 20 feet away. He came up and was observing again. "Would you like to take a little ride with me?" his mother asked. Mom had asked many times the day before, always with the same refusal: no. This time he surprised her and said yes.

Mom made it a short, successful run with a toboggan. Both rode together. He said yes when she asked if he liked it. "Do you want to do it again?" she asked. Again he said yes. They did two more runs and then rested. You can just imagine the expression on all our faces when we watched him pull the toboggan back up the hill on his own. Then he decided he wanted to go to the more challenging area of the hill and Susan stopped him for safety concerns.

Mother was very happy and grateful to see him become a part of the group and no longer be an outsider. We could see Ryder's expression of excitement at the thrill of the ride and, most of all, being able to join in with his peers and feel included. We were all amazed that Ryder was able to:

- Be brave enough to say he wanted to slide
- Coordinate his body in the snow to climb the hill the first time
- Successfully ride down the hill several times
- Desire to head to the more challenging section of the hill
- Pull the big toboggan on his own up the hill with confidence and coordination.

Linking Motor Development
To Academic Performance

How did Ryder's movement experiences of crawling and climbing all over the bunk beds affect his learning potential? Scientists have found that motor activities provide the sensory input to facilitate the brain with organizing the learning process. You have to do something before you have feedback that says you did it. In other words, as the spinal nerves develop, the motor nerves have the experience and myelinate first, before the sensory nerves can have the feedback. The body movements become a way to make the child more capable of performing motor skills, learning academics, and even influencing positive behavior.[5-1]

Motor control is important for the efficient use of energy. If all one's energy is used up controlling the body, there is none available to make memory impressions, and one must relearn things repeatedly. The ability to control one's movements is linked to having control over one's behavior. Many children who have poor body control also have very poor behavioral control. This is a common symptom of those children that have been labeled ADHD and ADD.[5-2]

Unfortunately, many times a child who has trouble learning is labeled "lazy," "oppositional defiant" or diagnosed as "autistic" or "hyperactive" (ADHD), when in fact, the problem is that the child's nervous system is not processing information properly. Children who have perceptual-motor deficits are unable to process information easily and to accurately learn. The nervous system is not firing most efficiently for seeing and hearing. Repetitive drills are not the answer for these children, nor will telling them over and over again to "try harder" or "sit still" or "pay attention." They are not intentionally disobeying the instructions. Their behavior cannot change without changing the way their nervous system is processing information. Medication is often used as a quick fix for controlling behavior, but it does not address the perceptual-motor deficit, and the learning problems remain.[5-3]

Mislabeling

Unfortunately, many times a child who has trouble learning is labeled "lazy," "oppositional defiant" or diagnosed as "autistic" or "hyperactive" (ADHD), when in fact, the problem is that the child's nervous system is not processing information properly.

A 6-year-old client named Ethan was unable to remember the letters of the alphabet and organize alphabet tiles in proper order. No matter how much repetition his parents or the teacher did with him with the alphabet, he just could not remember it. I facilitated Dr. Paul Dennison's brilliant and effective process called the DLR (Dennison Laterality Repatterning) with Ethan. In one session he was able to finally learn the alphabet, recite it properly, organize the alphabet tiles and store the 26 letters in long-term memory. The DLR allowed the information to become automatically remembered,

Chapter 5 Movement is the link to learning

and engaged both hemispheres of the brain and both sides of the body simultaneously.[5-4]

Basic Developmental Movement Patterns

Every movement has its roots in primitive reflexes and is connected with other movement patterns. At the foundation of child development are the primitive reflexes, righting reactions, equilibrium responses and the primary developmental movement patterns. These movement responses are automatic and are the basis for our movements of choice. Movement educator Bonnie Bainbridge Cohen developed these 16 primary movement patterns and calls them the Basic Neurological Patterns.[5-5]

The Basic Neurological Patterns are based on pre-vertebrate and vertebrate movement patterns. There are four pre-vertebrate patterns that entail movements also common to animals without a spine.

Cellular breathing is the expansion and contraction of every cell of the body, like the movement of one-celled animals. Cellular breathing is internal movement and underlies all other movement patterns of the body through space and postural muscle tone. Since every cell breathes, the whole body breathes, giving life to movement.

Navel Radiation is the movement of all parts of the body from our center core at the navel. There are 6 main parts comprised of the head, the tail and the four limbs. Navel radiation is the predominant pattern in utero for nourishment through the navel and movement from the core.

Mouthing is movement of the body starting from the mouth, then the head and then the whole body. The mouth is the first extremity to seek, reach, grasp, hold and let go. Mouthing involves rooting, sucking and swallowing and is the basis for nourishment after birth and articulating speech.

Pre-spinal movement is initiated by the spinal cord with the digestive tract.

The other 12 Basic Neurological Patterns are vertebrate patterns based on the following:

Spinal Movement is initiated from the head to the tail, like a fish, and tail to head. By placing babies on their stomach, they learn to initiate movement with their head and the spinal movement prepares them to rollover. Remember finding baby at the bottom of the crib? That's how they got there!

Homologous is the movement that starts from the two hands or the two feet simultaneously. This is the first pattern of locomotion initiated from the limbs. It is a symmetrical movement, like a frog jumping or jumping up to shoot a basketball.

Homolateral is the movement of two limbs on the same side of the body moving at the same time. A correlation is the movements of reptiles. The child is learning sidedness by shifting weight from one side of the body to the other – a hop, balancing on one foot and galloping. Eye-hand coordination, triggered by the Asymmetrical Tonic Neck reflex (ATNR), begins as hand-eye coordination when baby extends an arm to a toy after the head is turned.

Contralateral is the movement of one upper limb moving at the same

Developmental Movement Patterns
The building blocks of movement and understanding

Contralateral
Integrates all previous patterns;
foundation for crossing the midline.

Homolateral
Differentiates the right and left side of the body;
gains mobility.

Homologous
Differentiates the upper and lower halves of the body;
gains the ability to act.

Spinal Movement
Differentiates the front and back of the body;
gains the ability to attend.

Navel Radiation
Differentiation and connection.

Mouthing
First limb to seek, reach, grasp, hold and let go.

Breathing
Simplest ground of physical presence.

Sources: Adapted from *The Motor Development Across the Body Midline Student Manual* (1996) by Angelika Stiller and Renate Wennekes; and *Movement Exploration Student Manual* (1997) by Carol Ann Erickson, *Movement Based Learning For Children Who Have Special Needs* (2005) by Cecilia E. Koester and revised in *The SuperConfitelligent Child* (2007) by Denise Hornbeak

time as the opposite lower limb, as in creeping on all fours (crawling) and walking. The contralateral movement pattern is the foundation for all activities that cross the midline of the body, e.g., eating, dressing, reading, writing and sports. It activates both hemispheres of the brain and stimulates communication across the corpus collosum, the bridge between the two lobes of the neocortex.[5-6]

Movement Pattern	Movements	Plane	Differentiates	To Gain the ability
1. Navel Radiation	• Good night limbs	Horizontal and vertical	Limbs; upper from lower and side from side	To percieve movement & experience connectiveness
2. Spinal	• Rolling • Caterpillar	Horizontal	Front to back	To attend
3. Homologous	• Push-ups • Frog	Sagittal	Upper from lower	To act
4. Homolateral	• Alligator • Hop on 1 foot	Vertical	Right from left	To intend
5. Contralateral	• Crawl on all fours • Walk, run, leap	3-D movement	Diagonal quadrants of our bodies	To integrate attention, intention, action

Navel Radiation Activity – Good Night Limbs

Birth to age 10 – Good Night Limbs – While the child is lying in bed supine (tummy up), lay one of your hands on their navel (home hand) and from the navel move the other hand like an inchworm towards each limb and the head. As you are approaching each limb, call out that body part saying, "Good Night, right hand." The hand returns to the navel before setting out to say "Good Night" to another limb. "Good Night, left foot." "Good Night, nose."

Variation #1: Have them roll over on their tummy or, if they are very young and haven't started rolling, turn them over on their stomach. Now the home hand will be on their back in line with the navel. Move your other hand towards each limb again, including the head and also the tailbone.

Variation #2: Start with both hands at the navel and move them out simultaneously to two limbs, sometimes on the same side and sometimes on opposite sides, e.g., your right hand traveling to their left arm and your left hand to their right foot. "Good Night, left arm." "Good Night, right foot."

Variation #3: **Mouse Hunt for Cheese** - Whether on their back or tummy, call the navel or its back counterpart Home. From home run the "mouse" (fingers of one hand) to each limb in search of cheese. When you reach the left foot, move your fingers all around the foot and then up and down the sole of the foot and say, "Is the cheese hidden at the left foot?" Pause. "Oh, yes, here it is!" and smack your lips as if chewing. "Yummmmmmmmmm. Now let's take some cheese back home to your center." So then the fingers come scampering back to the navel.

Variations in the bathtub WITH CONSTANT SUPERVISION: Place the home hand on the baby's navel or back in line with the navel.

a) Drizzle water from a washcloth from the navel out to each hand, foot and up and down their midline.

b) Move a rubber duckie from the center of the body out to each extremity. Luke L., age 6 months, from Frisco, Texas loves it! Mom reports, "Now he finds it ticklish, which makes it even more fun."

With **Good Night Limbs** activities, baby is learning body parts and experiencing important tactile stimulation and navel radiation. Navel radiation is a reflexive movement pattern that develops at the same time as the primitive reflexes. It begins to develop the perception of movement, establishes the foundation for future patterns and connects all limbs to the core at the navel.[5-7]

A Moment To Explore For Yourself

Take a moment to lie on the carpet on your back, noticing the body breathing (**cellular breathing**). Did you feel your tailbone move as much as your head (**navel radiation**)? Rest a moment and then suck an imaginary shake through a straw. Swallow. Now flex your head a little, gather a little saliva from the sucking and see if it isn't easier to swallow with the head in that position. Next, leading with your mouth, turn your head to one side. Did you notice that ear perk up? Repeat on the other side, remembering to lead with the mouth (**mouthing pattern**). Next, on your tummy, wiggle your body like a fish forward and then backwards. Now roll over several times, experiencing your horizontal plane landing prone on your chest and stomach (**spinal movement**). Using both hands, push up to hands and knees and rock back on heels and push forward with feet to hands back and forward (**homologous movement**). Next, lie back down and crawl on your belly, moving one side then the other (**homolateral movement**). Lastly, push up to all fours and crawl around (**contralateral movement**).

Notice what happens when you let your leg lead first versus

when you let your opposite hand initiate the movement. What is the difference? Bonnie Bainbridge Cohen discovered that when a person started a crawl with a push of the leg, they went **homolateral**. When they initially reached with their hand, they went **contralateral**, giving them the whole-body integration experience.[5-8]

When the motor skills are developed, they provide the basis for the development of high-quality perceptual skills. The first information a baby receives about their world is sensed from the body's responses to the environment. The motor patterns will ensure that the child will obtain accurate and dependable information about their surroundings.

It is through these movement patterns that further neural connections are made between the balance mechanism of the vestibular apparatus and higher centers of the brain. Movement patterns for an infant involve the simple movements of flexing and extending the arms, which starts eye-hand coordination, and kicking the legs repeatedly for eye-foot coordination. The rolling at four and five months becomes the precursor for the balancing feats of sitting, rising to all fours, standing and eventually walking. When a baby starts to walk, a sense of freedom is created. The hands are freed up for carrying objects and the whole body is free to move independently. A whole new world of running, skipping, hopping, swinging and tumbling unfolds.

The brain has its own fixed schedule for maturation of motor pathways. Once the basic neural pathways are in place, their final function depends on practice. Neural connections are sparse at birth, but new connections are made at a remarkable rate during infancy, and by the age of six they are at maximum density. Thereafter, they decrease in a programmed cell death as unwanted connections die off in a process called apoptosis. People can increase neural connections throughout their life by learning new things and by movement, especially contralateral movement like walking. But if the brain is not used, the connections will become further depleted.[5-9]

A child, moreover, needs to have good motor development in order to have success on the playground and in sports, as well as school. It is also necessary for sensory integration, healthy self-esteem, social development and safety in this complex world.

Nurturing Moment

At age 5 Kevin was playing baseball with his Dad
out in the backyard. I was upstairs in my office and

when I looked out the window to watch him batting, I noticed that he was missing the ball most of the time. So I asked him to draw a Lazy 8 with the bat a few times. The next time his Dad pitched him the ball– Wham! The bat connected to the ball on the first swing, and he hit a home run out of the back yard and across the alley into the neighbor's plants.

To increase the development of a strong foundation, the infant needs an abundant quantity and quality of information being experienced starting in utero. Give the fetus and newborn many experiences of perceiving. To them, movement is perception. Move the pregnant body throughout many planes rising and lowering, twisting and turning, walking forward and back. Primary movements prenatally trigger brain development. After birth, parents can promote motor development by providing an unrestricted but safe place for exploration. Instead of saying, "No" frequently, parents can find the necessary environment so there is no concern for the child's safety or for objects breaking in the surroundings. Children need ample opportunity to move and play. By providing practice time for motor activity, children improve the movements and increase their interest and confidence in physical activity.

Children will blossom when given sufficient experience and early freedom of natural, physical movement. Today's generation

Primary Learning Tools
Promoting Motor Development

- Provide a safe environment for exploration
- Think twice before saying NO and DON'T so movement and play are free and unrestricted. Of course, supervision is always required.
- Provide practice playtime for physical, motor activity like crawling, rolling, running, jumping, climbing, hopping, skipping, sliding, tumbling and Angels in the Snow.
- Fingerplay — *Where is Thumpkin?*
    Eency, Weency Spider
- Circle games — *Motorboat, Motorboat*
    Ring Around the Rosie
- Make a fun obstacle course involving lots of crawling, climbing, jumping and side movement.

is sedentary in comparison to the "baby boomers" and preceding generations. It is critical for children to have more active movement like crawling, walking, running and climbing. Academic success depends on having visual, auditory and tactile skills in place. A child must first have the ease of lateral movement of the eyes as the precursor for reading, head-turning skills for listening and processing thoughts, and eye-hand coordination for writing, creative arts and sports. These are the preparatory, physical skills rather than the mental skills of learning.[5-10]

Nurturing Moment

When Kevin was 1½ years old and we were playing ball in the kitchen in the midst of preparing dinner, I noticed that he was being challenged to catch a rubber ball about 10" in diameter. He had no problem throwing it, but was missing it more than catching it. It's not unusual for a toddler who is just adjusting to being upright to have a hard time coordinating his eyes, hands and body to catch a ball. Being the Brain Gym Mom that I am, I had him put the ball down and do some Cross Crawls. I motored him through lifting his left leg and bringing his right hand over to touch it, and then lifting his right leg and bringing his left hand over to connect to it. After a few repetitions of Cross Crawling, his body incorporated the experience of the movement of crossing his midline. Then I tossed the ball at him again and he had no problem catching it. The rest is history. He loves all sports. He counted 23 different sports that, at age 9, he loves to play.

The Power of Play and Exploration

Movement is a child's first play. While children master organizing their body to become upright, and then sitting, standing, walking, running, walking on tiptoes, jumping, climbing and rolling on the ground, play consists of pure movement without a specific purpose. Children delight in movement for the pure joy of it.

Play is as essential as food and sleep for the developmental process of humans and animals. Some scientists judge it to be the most vital survival behavior: eliciting movement to grow the brain, heart coherence to enhance learning, touch through physical and verbal communication, and the all-important sense of belonging.[5-11] Play is a critical part of muscle growth and acquiring motor skills.

Rudolf Steiner, the prominent educator, scientist and visionary, observed that until children grow their permanent teeth, they live by imitation only. What they see daily, they reenact in their play.[5-12] Without discriminating, young children take in everything in their world, both physical and emotional. These impressions find their expression uncensored in their play. So if a child sees an adult repairing a toy with anger, the child will imitate not only the movement of repairing, but also the emotional mood and the verbiage that prevailed when the action was performed.[5-13] Those fuming words might come back to haunt or embarrass you! Innocent imitation is precisely why watching violence on television and playing violent video games is so detrimental.

True play is not meant to be highly structured nor competitive nor over-planned nor dangerous. Play emerges within a warm, protected and supportive environment with abundant parental involvement and an absence of a set goal except for the activity itself. Steven Siviy, a behavioral neuroscientist at Gettysburg College in Pennsylvania, found that when rats played, their brains released copious amounts of dopamine.[5-14] When children play, their brain releases this same neurotransmitter, dopamine. This chemical induces elation and exhilaration, and enables them to easily coordinate their actions. Dopamine organizes nerve net development and configuration all over the brain. When the dopamine levels of people with ADHD-hyperactivity and Parkinson's disease are measured, they register low. Consequently, natural play becomes a significant antidote to hyperactivity, learning disabilities and some diseases.[5-15]

Based on Jean Ayres' research, "the essential ingredient in play is the child's expression of his inner drive toward self-fulfillment as a sensory-motor being."[5-16] It is not the end result that makes the difference, but following the inner drive to master one's body and the environment. Physical movement generates sensory stimulation and adaptive responses that assist in organizing the brain.

A child obtains the sensory input from their body and from gravity through play. The sensory input, which makes it "fun," is necessary for emotional and motor development. Creative play is the way in which children familiarize themselves with the world. There are scores of recommendations for parents to create natural, simple games and activities for preschool children. Old-time favorite games like hide and seek, hopscotch and beanbag toss all develop sensory integration. Tricycles, bicycles, wagons, swings, slides, jump ropes and jungle gyms all move the whole body. Blocks, LEGO® Bricks and puzzles encourage children to manipulate things with their hands, thus developing complex nerve networks in the sensory and motor cortices of the brain.[5-17]

Carla Hannaford, Ph.D., proposes that parents use reality-based toys for children's play. For the young child, bring out the pots and pans, wooden spoons, whisks and scrubbers. Let the child explore soap bubbles and the feel of slippery dishes and utensils. Let the child's imagination run wild with sand, water, mud, sticks, seashells, birdseed and cardboard.

▲ **The music maker just needs a wooden spoon for his pots and pans.**

Participate with your child eating a variety of foods only with your fingers. The lips and fingers are two of the most sensitive parts of the body and also occupy a relatively large section of the sensory and motor cortices of the brain.[5-18] It is no wonder young children are always putting things in their mouth to learn about their world.

Joseph Chilton Pearce describes true play as "the ability to play with reality. True play drives imagination, gives resiliency, flexibility, endurance and the capacity to forego immediate reward on behalf of long-term strategies." [5-19]

Creative Play Activities

- Hide and seek
- Peekaboo
- Rolling balls on the floor to a partner
- Beanbag toss
- Hopscotch
- Tricycles
- Bicycles
- Wagons

- Swings
- Slides
- Jump ropes
- Balloons
- Jungle gyms
- Blocks
- LEGO Bricks
- Puzzles
- Drumming on pots and pans

▲ All it takes is a few cans and suddenly you are building towers.

Play Crawling

Just as the age of imagination and fantasy beginning at three years old is a crucial stage in normal development, crawling is an important part of physical development. Scientists concur that crawling is one of the key activities overall for infants. Crawling on hands and knees is the first movement of babies, which combines the use of the visual, proprioceptive and vestibular systems simultaneously as well as activating the Symmetrical Tonic Neck reflex.

Crawling is an important stage for developing visual perception. Through the act of crawling, the child learns how far away and how high objects are, how far to reach and how to maneuver the body out of tight corners. It enhances spatial

Reality-Based Play Toys

- Pots and pans
- Leaves
- Wooden spoons
- Soap bubbles
- Sand
- Mud
- Water
- Cardboard
- Cans for stacking
- Seashells
- Sticks
- Birdseeds
- Food

awareness, form constancy, knowledge of "self," independent achievement and so forth. The crawling stage lays down the neuro-motor patterns vital for child development.

Parents are counseled to keep babies crawling as much as possible in the first year and have them do cross-lateral movements in the midst of play in the preschool years. Locomotoring up and down stairs gives babies an opportunity to explore climbing in a supervised environment. Parents can pretend to be animals with their child and play chase on all fours. The kids love it and the sound effects are a big hit!

Children flourish when they are moving and playing. Children want to move because the sensation of movement nourishes their brain. It is easy for parents to provide many of these opportunities and they are forewarned of the detrimental effects of frequently saying No and Don't. The brain reacts much faster and much more appropriately when we instruct what we want done rather than telling or, worse yet, yelling what they shouldn't do. When we say "Don't hit your sister," the brain of a little child highlights the verb "hit" and continues hitting. If the hitting occurs, it's time to redirect the activity with a phrase like "Let's go swing." Find another activity to constructively utilize their energy and stir their imagination. Or perhaps it's time for a heart-to-heart and a good, strong hug.

> ## Play
>
> "Play allows for the development of a wide range of experience, so that what is first grasped through action can later be learned anew through thought."[5-21]
>
> — Rahima Dancy

As a parent, we must put aside our fears and own lack of abilities and motor control so our children may be empowered to use their own body and feel free to play and move. I know I had my apprehensions when my son wanted to start skateboarding. Going to the skate park was very frightening to me. I would catch myself holding my breath when watching one of the skateboarders drop down into the bowl, which looks like a big, empty swimming pool, or skateboard fast on the vert ramp. I recognized it to be my "stuff," my fear, and I supported him with encouragement just the same. When he is ready for the bowl and vert ramp, I will know he has had hours of practice. And it is a normal course of development to start with baby ramps and progress to that high-level stage. We have to be such conscious parents to be fully present for our children.

Teach every step of the way. Take time to supervise kids

when they are learning new things. The emphasis is on supervising instead of doing it for them. The more *they* can "do" while *you* are "being" and "playing" with them, the more new nerve pathways they are banking for future success and ease. Mistaking is learning. It is okay to make mistakes because it is part of the learning process.

The Primary Learning Tools (PLTs) offered throughout this book facilitate growth. A child must first have control of motion through activities like rolling, tumbling, somersaults and cartwheels before any child can have the attention for other experiences. Thereafter, the sensations of the other senses can fully integrate. Vision, hearing and the sense of touch are all linked to the vestibular system. Only when both motion and sensation are interwoven can the higher language skills of reading, writing and speech develop efficiently.

"Creativity and exploration are things that are good to let your kids do."

— Kevin, 9 yrs old

Making sense of the

senses

"Our senses give us information about the physical conditions of our body and the environment around us. Sensations flow into the brain like streams flowing into a lake. Countless bits of sensory information enter our brain at every moment, not only from our eyes and ears, but also from every place in our bodies."

— A. Jean Ayres

Generally speaking, a sense is a system by which outside stimuli in a physical energy form are perceived. We all learned in school the basic five senses of sight, hearing, touch, taste and smell which Aristotle originally described. Neurologists today do not agree on how many more senses humans have. Depending on the method of classification, between 9 and 23 senses have been identified including equilibrioception (the vestibular sense), proprioception (sense of one's body in space), thermoception (sense of heat and cold) and nociception (sense of pain).

The senses don't develop sequentially. One sense does not wait for another to be fully developed to start functioning. The body, like the brain, is holographic and intertwines in its growth like a beautiful symphony blending musical sounds together into one melodious whole. The entire body is developing simultaneously. It is just that different systems take the forefront at different times and some senses take longer to fully develop.

For the purpose of understanding a child's development, seven of the senses will be discussed individually in this chapter. Be mindful that these senses seldom function in isolation so there will be overlap in each section. They are the following: vestibular, tactile, olfactory, gustation, proprioception, hearing and vision.

Vestibular System

Why do children from the moment of birth love the sensation of motion? Why do they seek the slides, swings, teeter-totters and spinning equipment at the playground and swing from a tree or bar? The reason for youngsters' attraction to these movement activities is because they are born with a highly sensitive vestibular system, which gets activated with these movements. The vestibular system gives us our sense of balance and motion by sending messages to the brain about the position and movement of the head in relation to gravity. Then the body's movement and postural tone is modified to keep us upright. Gravity is the first challenge of muscle tone. Most vestibular activity functions subcortically so children are not consciously aware of this sense. They just know the resulting stimulation feels good.

We associate the ears with the vestibular system because the labyrinth of the inner ear houses not only the auditory organ called the organ of Corti in the cochlea (shaped like a snail shell) but the vestibular apparatus which includes the two types of vestibular sense organs: the semicircular canals and the otoliths. Movement of any type affects the three semicircular canals, especially rotational movements like spinning. There are two otolith organs: saccule and utricle. The saccule organ detects vertical acceleration, for example, in an elevator or amusement-park ride that drops you straight down. The utricle organ detects changes in horizontal movement, for example, when a car moves forward or when it slows down at a stoplight. All the vestibular sense organs are affected while on a roller coaster. It is a hair-raising ride in more ways than one.

The otolith structures themselves are small, dense, heavy particles composed of gelatinous matrix and calcium carbonate crystals. They are located in the viscous fluid of the saccule and utricle. The inertia of these particles causes them to stimulate hair cells when the head moves. The hair cells send signals down sensory nerve fibers, which are interpreted by the brain as motion.[6-1]

The formation of the vestibular system begins in the first month after conception. By five months in utero the vestibular apparatus, also known as the balance mechanism, has reached its full size and shape. The entire vestibular system is functioning in a mature way, providing that the pregnant mother has not taken any antibiotics called aminoglycosides, like streptomycin. They can cause permanent vestibular dysfunction and deafness.[6-2] When over-stimulated or damaged by ear infection, the vestibular system can cause motion sickness in a car, boat or plane, and dizziness on a dance floor.

Stimulation of the balance mechanism is an integral part of the embryo's growth from the time of conception and plays an important role in neurological and mental development. Since the vestibular system is the first to fully develop in utero, the embryo and fetus learn first through the perception of bodily movement.[6-3] Mother moves and the fetus makes adjustments to the change in position. The vestibulo-cochlear nerve, stemming directly from the vestibular system, is the first cranial nerve to develop at five to six months in utero.[6-4] It registers movement, position in space, velocity, vibration and two types of tone — sound and muscle tone.

The vestibular nerve is composed of 20,000 cells and sends impulses along the vestibular pathway from the semicircular canals of the inner ear to the brain stem, which is the hub or Grand Central Station from which information about balance, motion and all sensation is shuttled. Some vestibular fibers travel directly from the inner ear to the cerebellum bypassing the brain stem, thus reflecting the importance of balance in gross motor coordination.[6-5]

Benefits of Motion

Like the sense of touch, the vestibular sense transmits sensation for comfort and also for early brain development. The act of repetitive motion is very soothing to infants and young children. They even cry less if rocked, bounced, carried in a baby sling, jiggled upright in ones arms or when held over a shoulder and gently jiggled. When a baby is in a "disorganized" state with flailing limbs, tensing hands and face and crying in a high-pitch way, these activities can be extremely soothing. This applies to the similar behavior of a toddler having a tantrum. They are in such a disordered state that they need calming of the nervous system. Infants who are comforted through vestibular stimulation also show greater visual alertness than babies comforted in other ways.[6-6]

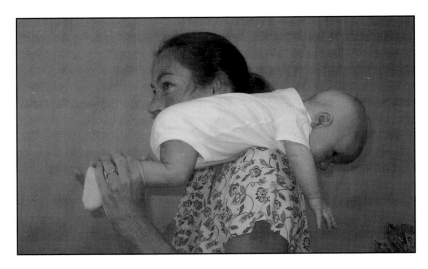

▲ **Gently giggle to calm baby**

The early onset of vestibular abilities is critical for the proper development of other parts of the nervous system. The sense of balance is intimately connected to the visual system and transfers to motor development. Any spinning activity elicits a rapid eye movement laterally upon cessation called nystagmus. One study found that a large portion of children with a deficient nystagmus response had delayed motor development for the critical motor skill of walking. Almost half the subjects were unable to walk by 1½ years and others only by 4 years.[6-7] Vestibular dysfunction may also cause emotional and perceptual problems, attention deficits, learning disabilities, autism and language disorders.

One study in particular by D. L. Clark (and others) substantiates evidence of the benefits of vestibular stimulation. The subjects were 3 to 13-month-old babies who were exposed to 16 sessions of chair spinning four times a week for four weeks. Each infant was seated on the lap of a researcher and spun around 10 times before an abrupt stop and a 30-second rest. Each session included one or two rotations in three positions to trigger maximum stimulation of the three semicircular canals in the inner ears. The striking results of the study showed more advanced development of both motor skills and reflexes for the treatment group. The results were most apparent with the motor skills of sitting, crawling, standing and walking.[6-8]

Since it is one of the earliest senses to mature, the vestibular system provides a large share of a baby's earliest sensory experiences. These experiences may play a critical role in organizing other sensory and motor abilities, which in turn influence the development of higher cognitive and emotional abilities. All the other senses that a child depends upon for learning are linked to the vestibular system of balance. These sensations pass through the vestibular system at the brain stem before traveling to their specialized regions in the higher centers of the brain.[6-9]

The most advanced level of balance is the ability to stay still. So what is the hyperactive child telling their parents and others around them? The boy or girl who constantly moves sporadically and skips and spins when told to walk is still in the process of learning to control their balance. The child who is always climbing all over the place instinctively knows that more practice for the vestibular system is required to properly develop. The body and mind are learning muscle and postural control, a sense of awareness of where the body's center is in space, depth perception and visual-motor integration skills.

According to Sally Goddard Blythe, a neurodevelopmental therapist, "Somersaults and cartwheels further facilitate the separation of motion from other sensations, for it is only when a child has control of movement that she can pay attention to other experiences." Goddard further stated, "Only when both motion and sensation are integrated can the higher language skills of speech, reading and writing develop fluently."[6-10]

For children who have suffered many ear infections as an infant and a preschooler, the whole balancing mechanism and vestibular system has been jeopardized. Have you ever closed your eyes when you had an ear infection and noticed how it threw your balance off? Ear infections affect the auditory, vestibular and proprioceptive senses. All the senses are intricately connected for the complex task of learning. Now let's take a look at some more activities to support the vestibular system.

Activities for Vestibular Activation

Most Brain Gym movements, in addition to other cross-lateral activities like walking and skipping, activate and develop the vestibular system. In particular, the Cross Crawl and the Elephant have this response in the brain, especially when moving slowly, and the Hook-Ups when standing. Through these movements new nerve pathways can be created to bypass any damaged tissue to and from the vestibular system.[6-11]

Cross Crawls are performed simply by moving one hand or elbow to the opposite lifted leg and then repeating with the other hand and leg. It is like the natural swing of walking. Cross

Crawls activate large areas of the two hemispheres of the brain simultaneously for crossing the visual/auditory/tactile/kinesthetic midline. The movement facilitates both eyes teaming together, improves hearing, and enhances coordination and spatial awareness. Children with their incredible creativity will come up with many variations of a Cross Crawl looking like monkeys, marching like a toy soldier, and imitating lions and tigers, etc.

▲ Kids love Cross Crawling

The Elephant, a very integrating activity, can be achieved by tilting the head to the side and relaxing the right ear on the right shoulder and pointing the right arm forward like an elephant's trunk. The hand and arm draw a big 8 on its side like the infinity sign. The whole body moves up and down, with relaxed knees, while the arm moves up in front of the midline of the body, toward the left and down on the left side, up the midline again and then toward the right side. Then it is repeated in the same way on the other side of the body with the left ear resting on the left shoulder.[6-12] The Elephant balances the Reticular Activating System (RAS). The RAS is the name given to the part of the brain believed to be the center of arousal and motivation. It is situated at the core of the brain stem between the medulla oblongata and the midbrain. RAS is critical in improving attention.

Neuroscientists are researching the relationship between the reticular activating system and various pathological conditions affecting behavior, such as Alzheimer's Disease. The RAS is believed to cause ADD and ADHD due to the imbalance of norepinephrine in the cells. This leads to the "hyper" and "lethargic" behaviors associated with these disorders.[6-13]

Vestibular Activities

- Swinging
- Rocking
- Bouncing on your lap
- Bouncing on a big ball
- "Trot, Trot to Boston"
- Turn baby upside down and jiggle gently from feet or over your shoulder
- Hopping
- Skipping
- Rolling
- Tumbling
- Climbing
- Somersaults
- Cartwheels
- Bike riding
- The Elephant
- The Cross Crawl
- Spinning in either direction to increase attention span
- Rhythmic Rocking

- **Trot, Trot to Boston** – Here's an old-time favorite: while child is sitting on your lap facing you, start bouncing your thighs and singing *"Trot, trot to Boston, trot, trot to Lynn* (Massachusetts), *watch out little girl* (boy) *you might Fall Innnnnnnn."* You are holding onto their hands or under their armpits as they bounce up and down on your lap. When you get to the last part, you spread your knees, so they drop down a little bit between your legs. They love this feeling of motion and the surprise feeling of weightlessness at the end.

The Academic World Starts Within

The vestibular system also gives us information to help us understand where we are in space. With this strong reference point, children will develop a physical foundation needed for mathematics and the figure-ground relationship to the whole, and perceiving and reading letters and words. A child must be able to know where they are, which is their body awareness, in relation to people and objects, in order to be capable of translating that to the two-dimensional world of paper, whiteboards and books. Different letters and words have similar shapes but are organized in different directions. A letter *b* can be seen with the round part on the right and the letter *d* with the round part on the left. This explains the reversals seen and heard when dyslexics read and write *was* for *saw* and *b* for *d*.

Children of all ages do their best learning during periods of calm alertness. During this time, they can most effectively absorb information about their world around them. Vestibular stimulation with the Primary Learning Tools suggested above provide this state of restful attentiveness for learning.

Touch: Tactile Perception

Touch is the sense of pressure perception, generally on the skin. There are millions of sensors in the skin detecting different pressures (firm, light, brushing, sustained, etc.) and temperatures (hot, cold, tepid, etc.), vibration and pain. In the developing fetus, the skin and nervous system both develop from the ectoderm, which is the outer layer of the embryo. The fetus responds to touch at a very early stage. At 5½ weeks an embryo can sense touch to the lips and nose. By the twelfth week, with the exception of the top and back of the head, all surface parts of the body respond to touch. There is an inherent genetic mechanism that protects the baby from experiencing the intensity of childbirth to the head.[6-14]

Tactile Defensiveness

If a child is tactilely defensive (hypersensitive to touch), their behavior will not improve with only vestibular stimulation until the touch sense is addressed first.

Touching (the expressive form) and being physically touched (the receptive form) are important for molding later tactile sensitivity, understanding the physical world and the ability to perform motor skills. It also affects a child's health, particularly their immune system, physical growth and their emotional well-being. In the womb, touch influences the developing embryo by triggering the withdrawal reflex and by stimulating physical development. Touch increases the release of Nerve Growth Factor (NGF), which stimulates and strengthens nerve development. Physical development in utero naturally occurs as a reaction to the force of the amniotic fluid and the uterus of the mother exerting pressure on the developing embryo.[6-15]

Mother love has a neurobiological basis that is essential for life. Research reveals that lack of sensory stimulation in the form of rocking and touching during the early stages of brain growth not only results in behavioral disturbances but also in brain damage to the neuronal systems that control affection. According to James Prescott, a developmental neuropsychologist,

"Substantial scientific evidence has documented the failure of maternal-infant/child affectional bonding as a major cause of depression, alienation, anger/rage, violence and substance abuse which is sought as self-medication for the emotional pain of loss of mother love and human love."[6-16] Prolonged separation of infant from mother can lead to sensory deprivation of tactile stimulation, physical contact and bodily movement, and cause structural, neuroelectrical and neurochemical alterations of brain cells.

Prescott additionally indicated that the social isolation and the deprivation in specific sensory and neurobiological processes of the vestibular and somesthetic systems were the basic cause of a number of abnormal emotional disturbances, including autistic behaviors like incessant rocking, hyperactivity, aggression, sexual aberration, drug abuse, violence and depressive behaviors.[6-17] The fundamental basis of Prescott's research and studies was derived chiefly by the landmark research of Harry Harlow and his wife, Margaret, at the University of Wisconsin in the 1950s and 1960s. The Harlows separated infant rhesus monkeys from their mothers and placed them in single cages in an animal colony room.

The rhesus monkeys were raised from birth with two "mothers." One surrogate mother was made of wire and the other was a cloth "mother" covered in terry cloth toweling. Half of the monkeys were fed by the cloth "mother" and half by the wire "mother." The feeding took the form of a nipple protruding from the chest connected to a supply of milk. The researchers recorded which mother the monkeys spent the most time clinging to, and measured their reactions when introduced to various objects, including a mechanical toy and a wooden spider. Frightened, they ran to "mother."

The findings concluded that all of the monkeys showed a strong preference for the cloth "mother," no matter which one fed them. All monkeys clung to her when frightened by the toy and spider, and returned to her after exploring the cage. The only time the monkeys ventured near the wire "mother" was to receive nourishment. The need for affection created a stronger bond between infant and mother than did the physical need for food.[6-18]

Here are my Top Ten Activities so your child can experience receptive touch and feel filled-up and whole.

1. Caressing, 2. Massaging, 3. Patting – Birth to 99 Years – All three are simple activities and usually well received. For some children the light touch of caressing has a stimulating effect so you will learn quickly the quality of the touch your child

Top Ten Activities for Receptive Touch

- Caressing
- Massaging
- Patting
- Squeezies
- Swaddling
- Carrying

- Burrito: Rolling in a blanket/carpet/gym mat
- Bean bag Chairs and Sofa Cushions
- Human Sandwich
- Pizza and Car Wash

needs under different situations. A firm touch is usually more appropriate initially with autistic and attention deficit hyperactive children to calm them, since they usually pull away from a gentle touch. After a while, that which seemed aversive to children with autistic or hyperactive behaviors becomes pleasurable and they will then seek out the tactile stimulation and physical contact. Your heart will sing when they open their arms to hug!

Developmentally, a firm, deep touch is more foundational in a child's growth than light touch. However, accepting light touch is key for being ready for performing fine motor skills in school, e.g., holding tools like pencils and crayons for writing and coloring. Even the light touch of a pencil is too much sensation for some children and alerts their survival response. Pencil grips make pencils fatter, which makes it easier to grip and gives some resistance, which is important proprioceptive (the sense of one's position in space) feedback.

4. Squeezies – Birth to 99 Years – With your thumbs lined up parallel to each other squeeze and hold, starting just above the ankles to go up the legs, and just above the wrists to go up the arms. The direction is always towards the heart. Apply just enough pressure to hold the limb and ask your child if they want you to squeeze tighter. The hands are covering as much of the circumference of the limb as possible and pressing for five seconds for children and seven to eight seconds for adults. Then move one hand-size up the limb. When doing Squeezies on the legs, include the hip by putting one hand above the pelvic bone and the other behind. When doing the arms also do the shoulders, pressing with one hand in front and one behind. This technique, called Tactile Embrace™ by Dr. Svetlana Masgutova, provides deep stimulation and sensory input to the legs and arms, helps concentration, satisfies the need for safety and is calming. If your child is sensitive to touch, you may do this procedure while they sleep. Many people instantly feel a calming effect within the first few squeezes.[6-19]

5. Swaddling and 6. Carrying – Infants benefit from being wrapped tight in their blanket like the nurses do with newborns at the hospital. Baby slings, and front and backpack carriers are wonderful options for touch stimulation and physical contact for baby. Babies love connecting, feeling your warmth and hearing your heartbeat. All these carriers provide hands-free access for preparing meals and other household activities as well as holding other children's hands while taking a walk or playing at the park. This swaddling effect of the blanket and the sling continues the experience in utero of the sense of solidness and identity. One thing to be mindful of with the front pack carriers is that they may be over-stimulating for very young infants, if they are facing out to the world. First preference is to connect heart to heart. Babies also love to be cradled and rocked.

7. Burrito – Many children, especially those who are hyperactive in their behavior and/or hypersensitive to touch, find it enjoyable and calming to be rolled up tightly in a blanket or piece of carpet large enough to cover from their neck to their feet and long enough so they can roll a few times. You can also use a small rug, but the carpet piece adds more tactile and pressure stimulation with its stiffness. Make sure the child has complete control of the whole process. The child must be in charge of the variables (whether to do it, when and where to do it, for how long, whether to have the head tucked in or out, whether the parent's hands are on or off after rolling up, and whether the hands are pressing steady or rocking). Most importantly, have the child be in charge of the amount of deep pressure you apply after they have become a Burrito. For their emotional well-being, it is critical they know

that you will stop applying pressure when they say so. Have them say *more, more* until the amount of deep pressure stimulation is just right for them. It is not nearly as effectual to rapidly push and release on their body. Make it is a slow, smooth, steady or

▲ **All rolled up tight**

rocking motion.

In some cases children may initially need to make the Burrito themselves and roll independently. Provide them with a blanket or quilt so they can roll themselves up and roll around on the floor as they see fit. At first they may roll around for 15 to 45 minutes to obtain the adequate pressure stimulation that their body is craving!

The Burrito activity relaxes tense muscles and calms the nervous system. In some cases it also positively affects the cerebellum and its sensory processing, and modulation of sensory input in several sensory modalities. The sustained, deep-pressure stimulation over a large area of the body is also a great technique for inhibiting tantrums.

8. Bean Bag Chairs and Sofa Cushions – Children crawl under a pile of sofa cushions or bean bag chairs, delighting in the pressure. Always supervise this activity.

9. Human Sandwich – Each child takes a turn being sandwiched between parents. They enjoy the experience of being the top bun too!

10. Pizza and Car Wash – Ask your child to lie down on their stomach in a comfortable place on a carpet, bed, grass or towel on the sand. Ask them questions to stir their creativity and find out the parameters of the kind of touch they want. It is important that the child has a chance to choose what kind of touch they will receive and to express when they have had enough. As with all these other touch activities, they must know that they are in charge and safe.

Follow with these kinds of questions. "Do you want to me to make you into a pizza or a car going through a car wash? Do you want the pizza (or car) to be only your back and shoulders or your whole backside including your arms and legs? What kind of pizza are you? What kind of crust?" (This will affect how much you press down the dough after it is kneaded.) "What do you want on it?" Once they have been kneaded and the crust formed and flattened, the tomato sauce and cheese are added if requested plus all the toppings. The tomato sauce is applied with your hands like two big paint brushes moving back and forth making a brushing motion. Now for the cooking – roll them in the oven and blow on them while they bake. After you roll them out of the oven, pick them up and pretend to eat them *Chomp chomp chomp* and *Yumm yumm yumm* with satisfaction.[6-20]

If they choose to go through the Car Wash instead, ask questions like "What kind of car are you?" "How dirty are you?" They will feel the imaginary soap you put on with your hands and the swishing of the brushes and the rinsing and the blowing dry.

Variation #1: They may prefer you to start with just their shoulders the first time or on their back for safe touch.

Variation #2: They can choose to be other foods like a salad, a banana split or a sandwich (the child is squished between two pillows).

Pizza and Car Wash are wonderful examples of receptive touch as well as full body play. Each allows for a lot of creativity and stimulates many touch receptors. The play of Pizza and Car Wash releases the neurotransmitter dopamine, leaving the child feeling more alert, elated and ready to explore. What a perfect way to bond with "the child heart" in kids and adults alike!

> **Taking Time to Touch**
>
> "The world will be a better place if Pizza and Car Wash catch on in each family."

Charlotte Palmer, an ESOL (English for Speakers of Other Languages) Resource Teacher of Pinellas Park Elementary School, states:

"This fall I started working with a speech-delayed 5-year-old boy named Frankie and his German mother from Tampa, FL. She feels he is an Indigo Child as she sees him as very intuitive. He's very high energy and is difficult to engage in anything but high-contact activities. I started doing tactile play with him like making him into a pizza based on William Steig's picture book, *Pete's a Pizza.* Carla Hannaford highly recommended this at 'The Physiological Basis of Learning' training I took with her in Tallahassee in October 2006. Since I started doing this, he doesn't want me to leave when our 90 minutes are up."

Pete's a Pizza is a picture book written and illustrated by William Steig, about a sulking, depressed youth that is cheered up when his father turns him into a pizza. Pete is kneaded and tossed like dough, adorned with checkers instead of tomatoes and thrown into the couch-oven, much to the boy's delight. Signe Wilkinson declared in *The New York Times Book Review* that "America will be a better place if the Steig family pizza party catches on." Yes, and I would add, "The world will be a better place if Pizza and Car Wash catch on in each family."

The Power of Touch

Receptive touch grows the brain and expressive touch does as well. From both tactile sensory experiences, those body parts sending the most electrical activity along their sensory fibers will establish the larger cortical spaces. Babies love to touch everything in sight because this gives them sensory input for which they will later be able to see that object and know what it is. Their hands, especially the fingertips, and their lips are programmed to develop many more sensors than other parts of the skin. It is these sensors, which send nerve impulses along nerve fibers to the somatosensory cortex of the brain, that will give babies invaluable information about their surrounding world and be crucial for their cognitive development.[6-21]

A baby begins to understand texture, temperature and shape by having the experience of touching objects or being touched by objects. A rock feels smooth, a cotton baby blanket feels soft and a piece of bark feels rough. A ball feels round to the touch, a banana is long, an unshaven face is prickly and the bath water is just right– just like in the womb!

Touch, even more so than any other sense, is readily accessible to young babies' and children's brains. How many of us just love holding babies? Touch offers the best and easiest opportunity for molding babies' ability to discern different tactile sensations (tactile discrimination), motor skills, mental abilities and emotional growth.[6-22] And it doesn't cost a dime; just your time.

Taste: Gustation Perception

Taste, also called gustation, is one of the traditional five senses and is categorized as one of the two main chemical senses. It is well known that there are four basic taste sensations on the tongue: sweet, salt, sour and bitter. But did you know that scientists now include a fifth receptor, unami, which detects the amino acid glutamate? Unami is a meaty, savory taste that drives our need for amino acids. The taste receptor cells in clusters are referred to as taste buds. The human tongue has about 4,600 taste buds on top of the tongue and another 2,500 interspersed on the epiglottis, oral and laryngeal pharynx and the soft palate.[6-23]

Each taste receptor conveys information to a slightly different region of the brain. The primary taste neurons release neurotransmitters and fire electrical signals along afferent nerves that run through the base of skull and into the first relay station for taste in the central nervous system, located in the medulla, triggering brain stem reflexes like salivation, tongue movement and swallowing. The medulla shuttles some information to the pons in the upper brain stem and to the thalamus. From the pons, taste inputs are relayed to the limbic structures, amygdala and hypothalamus that control motivation to eat and drink, and to the limbic cortex where the pleasurable aspects of taste are sensed.[6-24]

Activities for Taste Perception

Young children are imitators of our behavior. If we respond with a spontaneous *Yuck!*, don't be surprised or embarassed to hear that reaction by your wee one in a restaurant or at grandma's house. They are only being innocently honest in the moment. The more variety of foods children are exposed to when they are young, the more foods they will enjoy eating.

- **Two to Age 99** – Discuss and taste different foods with your children without judgement. Talk about the color and the texture, and how it tastes to them. Just because I don't like raw onions doesn't mean my son should be influenced by my aversion. Everyone's an individual and we all have our own preferences. It's fun to have some foods handy and take turns closing your eyes and guessing what food they put on your tongue. Each taste is a new experience, a new adventure!
- **Two to Age 99** – Expose your children to a variety of foods as this will influence their eating habits. A buffet restaurant provides an impressive array of colorful, tasty choices. A bite, here and there, of new foods will open up their food preferences.

We lived amongst many Mexican-Americans when Kevin was five and six years old. They all loved eating those *Hot Cheetos*®. He acquired a taste for hot, spicy foods and now he orders a level seven at the Thai restaurant. It's so hot it makes the hairs inside my ear canals stand up!

Smell: Olfactory Perception

The sense of smell, also known as olfaction and our olfactory system, is the other chemical sense and detects chemicals dissolved in air. Unlike taste, however, there are hundreds of olfactory receptors, each binding to a particular molecule. The chemicals themselves are called odors. Olfactory receptor neurons in the nose differ from most other neurons because they die and regenerate on a regular basis. The olfactory nerve for smell doesn't myelinate until birth, perhaps as a survival mechanism so the baby bonds with the mother and her milk.[6-25]

As discovered by Linda B. Buck and Richard Axel, mammals have about 1,000 genes for odor reception. Of these genes, 347 are functional odor receptors for humans. This amount was determined by analyzing the genome in the Human Genome Project. Buck and Axel were awarded the Nobel Prize in 2004 for this discovery. Each olfactory receptor neuron in the nose expresses only one functional odor receptor. Odor receptor nerve cells function like a key-lock system: only when the airborne molecules (the key) of a certain chemical can fit into the receptor (the lock), will the nerve cell respond.[6-26]

The olfactory system is our universal safety alarm. If we smell smoke, we are alerted to danger long before we may even see the fire or feel the heat. Sour milk never reaches our taste buds because the strong smell stops us from drinking it. Olfaction is our most reliable sense as it stays active 24 hours a day. We naturally smell all the time except of course when we cover our nose or when it is internally blocked.

Children make associations of smells that last a lifetime. Fresh baked apple pie or bread baking will trigger an emotional response to those that were exposed to those aromas as a child. Other scents elicit repulsive reactions. In some cases a child will use the sense of smell to identify objects quicker than sight. Others will walk outside the house and say, "It smells like spring."

Smell plays a major role in the perception of flavor. A simple experiment to demonstrate this point is to place peeled pieces of potato in one bowl and peeled pieces of apple in another. Now close off your nostrils with your fingers and sample a piece of each. Are you able to tell them apart? The taste of potato and apple are indistinguishable. We all notice food just doesn't have its delicious flavor when we have a cold and a stuffy nose.

Suggestions and Activities addressing the Olfactory System

- **Infant to Age 5** – Leave a piece of mother's clothing with the caregiver so baby or toddler can feel comforted by her smell.

- **Infant to Age 99** – Stimulating the olfactory system with fragrant foods, flowers and essential oils:

   1. Have your child sniff a lemon, orange, rose, jasmine or whatever fragrant foods and flowers you have in your area.
   2. *Furry stuffed animals* – Apply 1-2 drops of a familiar oil like lavender, lemon, peppermint, orange or rose onto each of the stuffed animals and leave to dry. Then put all the animals in a large box, big enough for your child to climb or crawl inside. Once they are in, ask them to find the

animal that smells like lemons, etc.

3. Play with *Scratch and Sniff* stickers and books.

4. *I Went to the Market* – Place several strong, smelling fruits and vegetables on a tray, e.g., grapefruit, passion fruit, banana, broccoli, oranges and lemons. With all players blind-folded, the first player takes an item from the tray, smells it and returns it to the tray saying, "I went to the market and I bought a lemon." Second player finds the lemon, smells it and puts it back. That player finds a new fruit/vegetable, identifies it and says, "I went to the market and I bought a lemon and a grapefruit." The third player smells the lemon, grapefruit and a new item. "I went to the market . . " and so on . . .[6-27]

5. Add a drop of lavender oil to a humidifier filled with water to run during the night, adding moisture to the air and a fresh, sweet aroma that is calming, relaxing and balancing. The body will get a deep, restful sleep, with the ears settled into the sounds of the white noise and the olfactory system sensing safety.

Proprioceptive Sense

Proprioception is the subconscious perception of body awareness and position in space. Sensory neurons, called proprioceptors, are located in the muscles and provide internal feedback to the brain of muscular activity. These proprioceptors may be described as "the eyes in the muscles of the body." They send information about changes in muscle length, tension and muscle contraction levels to the spinal cord and the cerebral cortex so you perceive in every millisecond where a body part is and can make adjustments accordingly.[6-28]

With good proprioception a child will be able to sense the position, stability and movement of their muscles, joints and tendons. Assuming all other sensory systems are intact, the child will not bump into furniture, be clingy or have difficulties with activities like standing on one foot or walking a rope with eyes closed. All systems work together synergistically to provide awareness, direction and orientation in relation to nearby environmental objects.

Through our proprioceptive sense we unconsciously develop our sense of boundaries: where we begin and end. Receptors in muscles and joint-supporting ligaments, as well as in the skin, relay information to our nervous system. Close your eyes and touch your nose. Clasp your hands behind your back. Now think, is your left or right thumb on top? It is our proprioceptive system that knows where our nose and thumbs are, and along with our kinesthetic memory, accomplishes these tasks with ease. It is our proprioceptive system that perceives this kinesthetically, working in beautiful harmony with the other sensory systems, which provide their supporting roles.

Another simple demonstration to become consciously aware of your proprioception is to close your eyes and wave your hand around. Assuming proper proprioceptive function, at no time will you lose awareness of where your hand actually is, even though your hand is not being detected by any of the other senses.

Activities to develop the Proprioceptive Sense

Children with an inefficient proprioceptive system may appear clumsy and uncoordinated, may have difficulties controlling the movement of a pencil, crayon, etc. to write or draw and may chew on pencils, pens, gum or their shirt. When you observe these symptoms, they are sending you a SOS that neurologically their proprioceptive sensory system has not matured or the Rooting and/or Sucking reflex has not integrated. They need more sensory input with deep-pressure stimulation at their joints.

Provide them with:
- A chew tube on a string or cord so they can wear it like a necklace when not in use
- Crunchy foods (stimulate alertness and/or release anger)
- Gum to chew
- Thick liquids to suck through a straw
- Chewy foods like gummy bears for organization

Activities
- Yawning and stretching together like cats
- Crawling through tunnels
- Climbing in trees, up ropes, in play structures
- Swinging across monkey bars and hanging from them
- Deep pressure down the sides of the spine (see Back Roller, Tension Tamer number three page 40 in Chapter 3.
- Wheelbarrow walking with an adult holding the child's legs

Hearing: Sound Perception

Hearing is the primary route for speech development and language acquisition. Because language is the main means used to teach children, hearing is one of the most important senses for their intellectual growth. Children's early exposure to music and speech are immensely vital in shaping many higher aspects of brain function, including language, emotion and other cognitive abilities.

The Biology of Hearing

Hearing, also known as audition, is the sense of sound perception. It results from tiny hair fibers in the inner ear detecting the motion of the tympanic membrane (commonly known as the eardrum) which vibrates in response to changes in the pressure exerted by atmospheric particles within a range of 9 to 22,000 Hz. Humans can distinguish over 400,000 different sounds. It is the sensors in the coiled cochlea of the inner ear that detect these sounds after the sound waves have traveled through the ear canal, causing the eardrum and the three tiny bones of the middle ear called ossicles to vibrate. The three bones— the stapes, the incus and the malleus— amplify the sound waves. The electrical activity of auditory stimulation refines the neural connections between the thalamus and cerebral cortex. Auditory fibers make their way from the thalamus axons to the auditory centers of the cortex. The ears may be the sensory organs for hearing but, ultimately, it is the brain which must process and make sense of the sound perceptions sent from the ears.[6-29]

Early Auditory Development

Sound perception miraculously transpires for the first time the day after the first heartbeat in gestation. The human heart begins to beat and pump blood around day 22. An embryo begins to react to sound 23 days after conception.[6-30] By the 23rd week the fetus responds to loud, mid-to-low pitch sound stimuli with the startle response generated by the Moro reflex. In the last trimester, the fetus primarily hears bass sounds of low frequencies and deep male voices. Additionally, there is auditory perception of mother's voice, her heartbeat, blood flow and stomach gurgling.

This act of hearing influences the quality of auditory development, and all the listening that children experience from the third trimester on significantly shapes the way their brain becomes wired to process and understand different sounds. Beginning in the womb, every subtle aspect of a child's

---

early auditory experience is affecting hearing development. Researchers studied babies whose mothers read to them during the last six weeks of their pregnancy. The fetus was read Dr. Seuss' *The Cat and the Hat* twice a day for a total time of approximately 5 hours during the six-week period. When tested shortly after birth, the babies sucked more while nursing to the reading of this familiar story instead of *King, the Mice, and the Cheese*. This study proved that babies do imprint on auditory experiences while still in the womb.[6-31]

After birth, babies recognize and prefer *parentese* baby talk starting at 5 weeks old. Their most sensitive frequency range is high pitch starting at 3 months old. *Parentese*, also labeled *motherese*, is optimally stimulating to a baby's hearing especially when it is slow, high-pitched, highly intonated speech and accompanied with affection.[6-32]

A Baby's early experience with language profoundly and permanently influences the range of speech sounds they will later be able to perceive and to speak. The variety of music or natural sounds children are exposed to makes a difference in whether they end up with a more discriminating ear for things like perfect pitch, or perhaps an ear for birdcalls. Auditory development remains malleable throughout preschool and the early grade school years while the synaptic wiring is still being refined.

"Risk Management" for Hearing Impairment

Factors influencing the proper development of the hearing apparatus include prenatal infections, especially German Measles (rubella) and CMV (cytomegalovirus), drugs (particularly antibiotics, loop diuretics, anticonvulsants, anti-thyroid drugs), chemicals like nicotine and alcohol, and environmental toxins like mercury and lead. Some of the perinatal factors to consider are birth asphyxia (abnormally low oxygen levels), bacterial meningitis and jaundice. Because bacterial meningitis inflames the brain's membranes, it can damage virtually every site in the auditory system, from the inner ear to the auditory cortex.[6-33]

Three major risks for a much higher rate of hearing impairment are a low birth weight, a premature birth and chronic ear infections. Statistics indicate that eighty percent (80%) of all children will be diagnosed with at least one middle ear infection before they are 3 years old. Antibiotics cure only one in seven children with acute otis media (middle ear infection). Eighty-one percent (81%) of ear infections heal over time without pharmaceutical treatment. There are at least three factors that can reduce the propensity for ear infections.

1. Breast feeding, especially when mother's milk is baby's exclusive nourishment for the first 4 months. Breast-fed babies are only half as likely to get multiple ear infections as bottle-fed babies. The advantage is related to a factor in the milk that protects the baby up to 3 years. Making it the only source of milk for the first 6 months improves its effectiveness.
2. Eliminate second-hand smoke. Children exposed to smoke have forty percent (40%) more ear infections.
3. If possible, make it a point to avoid daycare centers for the first 18 months. One study revealed that children 18 months and younger in group-care situations were seven times more likely to need ear tubes then those cared for at home.[6-34]

Historically, screening for hearing loss included testing only infants identified at high risk, but ninety percent (90%) of hearing-impaired infants are born to normal-hearing parents, and less than half of hearing-impaired infants have known risk factors. Currently, recommended practice begins with Universal Newborn Hearing Screening (UNHS), where every newborn is screened at birth for hearing loss. The goal of UNHS is early identification and intervention, including hearing aids when appropriate before six months of age, preferably no later than three months. This achieves the goal of both the Joint Committee on Infant Hearing (JCIH) and the American Academy of Pediatrics (AAP) of early intervention by six months of age. Recent research concluded that children born with hearing loss that were identified and given appropriate intervention before six months of age had significantly better language skills than those identified after six months of age.[6-35]

Educational Difficulties Based on Hearing Impairment

The symptoms of auditory problems can manifest in difficulties reading aloud, speaking, poor reading comprehension, poor spelling, short attention span, an inability to follow a series of instructions in sequence and a limited vocabulary.[6-36] Early detection of a hearing impairment is crucial to prevent unnecessary challenges learning in school.

Hearing loss is detrimental in the following significant ways:
• It causes delay in the development of the communication skills of speech and language.
• The language deficit causes learning problems that result in reduced academic achievement.

- Communication difficulties often lead to social disparities of isolation and poor self-concept.
- Hearing loss may have an impact on vocational choices.

The Role of Auditory Discrimination

Anthony Storr, a distinguished English author and psychiatrist, discussed two essential components for reading: 1) hearing and 2) vision. He referred to the "auditory reader" as one who not only reads phonetically but also sees and hears the words inside his head, as if they were being read aloud. If a child has difficulty discriminating sound, this process will be impeded.[6-37]

Tone it down

By keeping traffic noise and the volume of a radio and television to a minimum, children can pick up on important auditory cues rather than having their auditory system become overwhelmed.

During the first three years of life, children must learn to use their ears to "tune-in" to the specific frequencies of their own language, like tuning to a radio station. The ability to discriminate sounds in a noisy background is very poor for young children up to age 10. The background noise masks the sounds of interest, making them obscure. A continuous disharmony of background noise in childhood or a lack of auditory stimulation can discourage early listening and the child at an early age learns to block out and ignore sound.[6-38]

By keeping traffic noise and the volume of a radio and television to a minimum, children can pick up on important auditory cues rather than having their auditory system become overwhelmed. Creating an auditory environment where they are listening to one thing at a time is particularly important when they are learning the subtleties of speech.

Acquisition of Speech Sounds

According to licensed Speech Language Pathologist, Jean Bowlus, M.A., CCC-SLP, there is a developmental sequence for the acquisition of speech sounds (phonemes) by children. Within this developmental sequence, there is a range as to what is considered within normal limits regarding the actual sequence and age that the speech sounds are acquired by a given child. Phonological development is defined as the ability for a child to accurately produce the speech sounds in their given language, and occurs over a number of years. Some normally developing children complete their phonological development earlier and others later. Typically, vowel sounds are all acquired by three years of age. The acquisition of some consonant sounds, normally, begins to occur in infancy along with the acquisition of the vowel sounds. The vowel sounds and the consonant sounds /p/, /b/, /m/, /w/ and /h/ are, statistically, amongst the earliest speech sounds acquired in the English language. From statistical analysis, some of the latest consonant sounds to be acquired by English speaking children include, but are not limited to: /r/, /l/ /s/, /z/, /th/ and /v/.

A speech pathologist at the local elementary school can provide parents with specific information as to which speech sounds are age-appropriate for their toddlers and young children, and which speech sounds may be considered developmentally beyond the age of their children.

If parents are concerned about their children's hearing, speech and/or language development at any age, it is recommended that they consult their pediatrician. Additionally, for parents with children at age three or above that have questions in these developmental areas, it is recommended that they contact the Speech Language Pathologist at their local public school. Speech Language Pathologists in the public school setting will typically screen children at age three and above in the areas of hearing, speech and language. Parents may request a screening test for their children by a Speech Language Pathologist in their school district, and the children who don't pass the screenings in one or more areas will be recommended for further evaluation in the area(s) failed. For parents with concerns in the areas of hearing, language and/or speech in their children who are under the age of three, it is recommended that they consult their pediatrician and, also, consider contacting the Director of Special Education in their local school district for information regarding available agencies that provide evaluation and treatment services for children under the age of three. The earlier a problem is identified and treated, the better it is for the child's development.[6-39]

Learning Foreign Languages

The window of opportunity for learning a foreign language is optimum in the first three years of life while the ears are making their fine-tuning adjustments. Children learn to filter out unnecessary sounds and tune in to the sounds of language.

Through this auditory discrimination they can start to hear and reproduce the sounds necessary for speaking and, later, for writing.[6-40] By hearing your voice in as many languages as you know, babies will learn about the sounds of language that they will soon be imitating.

Activities for Better Auditory Processing

Parents can support auditory development with their children prior to kindergarten with many activities. The main activities are to read daily, speak often, and expose them to different sounds and different types of music.

Auditory Activities

- Read and speak with your children frequently
- Expose young children to different sounds
- Encourage Baby's vocalization
- Megaphone

- **Read and Speak with Your Children Frequently** – The nighttime reading ritual will have your child saying, "Again, again!" They are fascinated with the magic of listening to storytelling. Ask them questions to stimulate their imagination, thought and speech. "What do you suppose happened next?" "What was she doing?"
- **Expose Young Children to Different Sounds**– Playfully explore listening to sounds you hear in nature (rain falling, leaves rustling in the wind or leaves being crushed with little and big feet, birds chirping) and exclaiming speech sounds with vocal play ("ah," "eeee," "mmmm," "baa, baa.") Start with vowel sounds and the consonant phonemes /p/, /b/, /m/, /w/ and /h/ for they are the easiest for babies to pronounce. Toddlers have a more difficult time articulating "rrrrr," "sssss," "th," "la la," "zzzzzz," the hard sound of a /k/ and consonant blends, so even though it is important for them to hear you say words with those speech sounds, be patient with their replication of them. Most young children are not developmentally ready and should not be expected to produce phonemes that are beyond their developmental age.

Interestingly enough, the /s/ sound, like a snake makes, comes from the back brain and doesn't require the vocal cords. Avoid using the s buzz sound with children with autism, ADHD, fear phobias and cerebral palsy because their movement system is not developed enough to escape. Even snake and dinosaur toys, straps, strings and rubber bands can activate the brain stem of some children for a survival reaction and protection.[6-41]

Caution: A pacifier changes the construction of the mouth palate and interrupts natural resonation of sound. Infants and toddlers need to hear parents, siblings and others speak to them directly.[6-42]

- **Encourage Baby's Vocalization** – Let baby know you love to hear them talk and sing even if it just sounds like babble to you.
- **Megaphone** – it is important for children to hear their own voice. Have a child talk or sing into a microphone or cut the bottom of a plastic gallon water or milk jug so they can hold the handle and put the open bottom up to their nose and mouth. They will be able to hear their own voice, which is a precursor to reading.[6-42]

Auditory Games

- Drum Game
- Clapping-Tapping Game
- The Elephant
- Thinking Caps
- Bop-It

- **Drum Game** – to develop the auditory and motor system. The parent stands behind the child so the drumming cannot be observed. With a small drum, the mother or father taps out simple patterns and then passes the drum to the child to repeat the pattern. A variation is to clap out the pattern or use two wooden sticks or spoons instead of using the drum. Progress to more complicated patterns and add background music or noise to improve the auditory figure-ground skill.
- **Clapping-Tapping Game** – to integrate the auditory, visual and motor systems. Show the child claps (C) several times and label it clapping. Demonstrate taps (T) by tapping the table where the child is seated with both hands. Begin with simple patterns.

Say, "We are going to play a clap and tap game. I will do it first. Watch me carefully and then I want you to do it."

1. CT (a Clap then a Tap)
2. CTC (Clap, Tap, Clap)
3. TTCT
4. CC-T (a hyphen signifies a two-second pause: Clap, Clap, two-second pause, Tap)
5. T-TT
6. TCTTC

7. CT-TC

8. T-CTC

9. CCT-T

10. T-C-CT

Give the child several opportunities to practice the more complex patterns.[6-43]

- **The Elephant**– described in the Vestibular section above on page 82, also activates the brain for crossing the auditory midline, thus affecting the auditory skills of recognition, discrimination, perception and memory.[6-44]
- **Thinking Caps**– Unfold the curly part of the ears starting at the anterior part of the top of the ears with the thumb and index finger. Unfolding all the way down to the ear lobes. The Thinking Caps activates the brain for auditory attention, recognition, discrimination, memory and perception.[6-45]

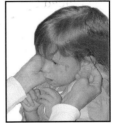

Rhythm, Beat and Hearing

Another aspect related to hearing is sound and, most specifically, the sound of a heartbeat. As stated by Carla Hannaford, Ph.D., the human heartbeat is such a strong pattern that a fetus will respond to drumming at 25 weeks after conception. Steady beat is basic to the love for music with a beat. It assists the organization of such bodily movements and functions such as walking, breathing and dance patterns. In checking preferred drum rhythms worldwide, the one most frequently favored is the coherent beat of the human heart.

Activities to instill a steady beat

- Rocking
- Patting with a steady beat
- "Pat-a-cake, Pat-a-cake"
- Nursery rhymes
- Children's songs
- Tapping on a child's back
- Rhythm Cups

The steady beat underlies our ability to pick up the pattern of language, express it as verbal language and translate that pattern to symbols for the capacity to read the language. Many of today's children are deficient in steady beat competency. In 1998 Dr. Phyllis Weikart tested elementary school children for their steady beat competency. The results indicated that less than ten percent (10%) of the students exhibited the ability to maintain a steady beat. Normally this ability is in place by 2-3 years of age for adequate linguistic development.[6-46]

Children naturally love to be rocked while snuggled up against a soft body and listening to the rhythm of the heartbeat. As stated by Carla Hannaford, Ph.D., "If the mother's heart rhythm is coherent, it forms the framework for our ability to maintain a steady beat pattern throughout our lives."[6-47]

- **Rhythm Cups** – With one plastic cup for each person in play, have everyone sit around in a circle "criss-cross applesauce." Knees are almost touching the people to each side. Each cup is placed upside down in front of each player. Music is added for enjoyment. The two routines are as follows:

Routine 1: *8 counts*
   1. Pat floor on outside of cup with both hands
   2. Clap hands
   3-4. Tap cup 3 times with fingers, alternating hands (R-L-R or L-R-L)
   5. Pat floor on outside of cup with both hands
   6. Clap hands
   7-8. Pass the cup to the right (counter clockwise), placing it on the floor in front of your neighbor

Routine 2: *16 counts*
   1-2. Pat floor 2 times
   3-4. Clap hands to neighbors 2 times
   5-8. Snap fingers in air 4 times
   9-10. Pat floor 2 times
   11-12. Clap hands 2 times
   13-14. Snap fingers in air 2 times
   15-16. Pass the cup to the right (counter clockwise), placing it on the floor in front of your neighbor

The objective of Rhythm Cups is to instill a steady beat, improve coordination, peripheral vision, spatial awareness and teamwork.[6-48] This is an excellent movement activity for transition in the classroom.

Celebrating Sound through Music

A great way to celebrate sound and the development of listening skills and languaging is through music. Music is one of baby's first natural teachers. The fetus responds to music with changes in motor activity. Listen to a baby coo. Doesn't it sound like singing? Isn't it melodious? Toddlers and preschoolers love listening, singing along and dancing to traditional songs. Kids of all ages love the joy that music brings to their life.

Expose Children to different types of music

- Listen to jazz, country, rock-n-roll, classical music, etc.
- Dance and sing with your child to kids' music. There are singers/musicians that have written and/or performed music for the children of the world. Raffi, Jane Austin, Greg and Steve, Karl Anthony, Shaina Koll and Jim Valley, to name a few, each have a great selection of children's music.

Kindermusik® is a brilliant program for young toddlers and preschoolers to experience with a parent. Their philosophy, founded upon extensive research, is in alignment with my own:

- Every parent is the child's most important teacher.
- Every child is musical.
- The home is the most important learning environment.
- Music nurtures a child's cognitive, emotional, social, language and physical development.
- Every child experiences the joy, fun and learning which music brings to life.

Another program for young children, as well as elementary school students, is Education Through Music® (ETM). It is a linguistically based program where traditional songs, movement and interactive play are designed to promote simultaneous emotional, social, cognitive and musical development. ETM fosters the well-being and development of children and their caregivers.[6-49]

The Wonders of Hearing

Excellent hearing is much more than the ability of the ears to detect sound. The connections between the ears and the neural circuitry are responsible for the finer levels of auditory discrimination e.g. a musician's trained ear to discern whether their instrument is in tune or an ornithologist distinguishing different types of birds by their calls. Can you pick the different instruments out of a song? People with highly developed hearing can do so, and they have the same ears as you do. The difference is not your ear but in the way that different auditory experiences have shaped your neural circuitry to process the sound information coming into your brain. You are not required to be a musician or ornithologist to need good auditory processing.

As is beautifully summarized by Sally Goddard:

" Sound is vibration, motion and energy. If we hear no sound we perceive danger, for the totally silent world is a dead world. Sound passes through all levels of the brain, affecting not just the ear and the vestibular but also our bodies through bone conduction. The significance of sound for learning is immeasurable." [6-50]

Seeing: Visual Perception

It is generally recognized that 80-85% of learning comes through the eyes. The eyes are, however, so much more than light receptors. They are an integral part of the central nervous system. Sight is referred to as one of our senses, but vision includes the whole process of transmitting visual impulses to the brain after the eyes have received the light on the retina. The brain makes the interpretations of the visual impulses and decides how to respond to them via the motor system. Vision influences, and is influenced by, the movements of the whole person. A demonstration of how vision influences bodily function is experienced by standing on one foot and looking straight ahead. Then observe what happens to the whole body when the same activity is performed with eyes closed.

Vision is an integral part of a child's whole development. As the rest of the body is developing, so are the eyes. The visual skills a young child learns provide the foundation for later visual complexities. Poor visual skills can lead to difficulties with learning, overall school performance and sports. Without visual-perceptual processing, a child would be incapable of accurately learning to read, copy from the board or from a book, give or get directions, remember things visually, visualize objects or past experiences, and have good hand-eye coordination. The ability to integrate visual information with the other senses is needed to play ball, ride a bike or hear a sound and be able to visually recognize where it is coming from (like a train).

Are We Harming Instead of Helping?

Are today's toddlers and preschool children allowed to let their eyes and vision develop naturally through play and exploring their world? Or are they being forced into two-dimensional near- point activities such as reading and writing, and prematurely using electronic games, computers and television? Vision is the result of a complex sequence of connections and neural developments that typically take place in the early, impressionable years and is contingent upon adequate maturation of the central nervous system.[6-51] Given the importance of the development of healthy vision to a child's ability to learn, it is worth thinking about how prolonged exposure to two-dimensional visual processing affects young children.

Most public schools now want children reading by age five. Is this really healthy? Some experts say the eyes are not physiologically developed for reading until age seven or eight. When the frontal lobes of the neocortex mature, the muscles throughout the body, including the eyes, will be able to perform fine motor activities in a coordinated way. The frontal eye field of the frontal lobes needs to be mature enough in order for the accurate eye-teaming required by the two-dimensional focus of reading to occur.[6-52] One reason for concern is that by forcing the eyes to do something they are not ready for, we are setting up children for eyestrain, myopia and other visual problems.

Another large source of two-dimensional visual processing for young children is electronic media. With the advent of the technological revolution and a plethora of computer software for children, many parents deem it necessary to make their children computer literate by three years old. Some parents believe that learning how to read and do arithmetic on the computer will provide their preschooler with an advantage for future academic success. Research, however, does not show this to be true.

Jane Healy, an educational psychologist, reviewed hundreds of studies on the effects of computers for educating young children. Healy concluded that there is **no advantage at all** for children six and younger to use computers. Sadly, there are significant disadvantages, both physical and social. Physiologically, there is a potential risk for eyestrain, loss of visual acuity, carpal tunnel syndrome and the potential effects from electromagnetic radiation emissions. Because computer applications are designed to be so visually and behaviorally engrossing, computer use subverts youngsters' natural instincts for physical play, social interaction and creativity.[6-53]

The Role of Experience on Visual Acuity

Another important implication of prolonged visual processing in the two-dimensional field is how it may affect a child's visual wiring in the brain. Researchers have shown that very subtle variations in a child's early visual experience have a long-lasting impact on their visual circuitry and perceptual abilities. Further, early experience critically shapes a child's skills of hand-eye coordination, observation and spatial perception. Since most young children are reared in houses and apartments, giving them primarily vertical and horizontal stimuli, they have slightly better acuity for these two orientations. By contrast, in a study of Canadian Indians, Blakemore & Cooper found that these Canadian Indians had greater acuity for angles since they had been raised in the traditional teepees. Because of their surroundings, they had more cortical neurons that detected oblique angles in space. A child needs to experience the different directions– horizontal, vertical, diagonal (orientations of lines and objects)– in their environment in order to create the visual wiring for this perception.[6-54] Note that these skills are absolutely necessary for both reading and math.

The work of Nobel Prize winners David Hubel and Torsten Wiesel in the 1960s was even more dramatic. Working with kittens and monkeys, these neurobiologists discovered that visual experience directs the wiring of the visual brain. They sutured shut the eyes of infant animals during the period when the brain is normally establishing contact with and learning to interpret visual input from the eyes. When deprived of visual experience, the animals failed to develop appropriate visual circuitry in the brain. Even though they had perfect eyesight, the animals were functionally blind.[6-55]

Developmental Stages of Vision

An infant initially understands an object in their world by orally touching it with their mouth and tongue. Then at 6-12 months, once fine motor skills have been established and the baby can crawl, the perception of form is experienced additionally by locomotoring to the object and exploring it with the fingers. Eventually, by 12-15 months when the eye muscles start to coordinate with each other, form perception and the sensory input shifts primarily to the eyes. Toddlers recognize objects from a distance based on past experiences. They no longer have to touch the object to see it. At this stage they can just look.

Compared to the other senses, vision is still primitive at birth. Newborns see clearly 8" in front of them, but essentially see better peripherally. By six months all primary visual abilities will have emerged: depth perception, fine acuity, color vision and eye movement. Despite the fact that visual development begins 22 days after conception with the first optic tissue, it takes years before all of the eye's pathways are firmly stabilized.[6-56]

Brain stem circuits are responsible for most newborn visual skills, including blinking, dilating of the pupil, eye movements and the ability to track a slowly moving object. The movements are jerky saccades, a reflexive form of eye movement. By two months the tracking shifts into the cerebral cortex and becomes smooth movement providing the vestibular system developed fully in utero.

Visual abilities are highly malleable until age two, and somewhat less so until eight or nine years of age while synaptic pruning is occurring. Normal visual input to the brain is essential to achieve normal wiring in the visual cortex. The eyes are literally competing for synaptic space in the visual cortex. Electrical activity is mandatory to develop binocular neurons for depth perception and high acuity to detect detail.

As with hearing, a childhood synaptic pruning, called apoptosis, occurs with vision, beginning around age two. Forty percent (40%) of the dense visual cortex synapses are eliminated during a long period extending through childhood. Myelination, a forming of an insulating fatty covering of the nerves, continues also during this time. The connective tissues of the eyes are still developing until seven to eight years old. Synapse refinement continues to eight years old, so acuity and binocularity stay vulnerable throughout the preschool years.

Preventing Visual Problems

The educational system simply examines children in school for their distant visual acuity. Academic success requires much more sophisticated analysis to discern where the gaps exist when a child is faced with an inability to read, to write or to spell. Visual-perceptual, visual-motor integration, oculomotor and directional awareness skills are as fundamentally important for learning as seeing clearly at a distance.[6-57]

It is estimated that five percent (5%) of preschoolers in the United States have a vision problem that will ultimately lead to a severe learning disability or, worse yet, unnecessary loss of sight. Forty percent (40%) of grade school children are visually impaired for satisfactory school achievement.[6-58]

A child's visual system is checked initially at birth for any congenital eye problems. The American Optometric Association recommends that babies have their first comprehensive eye assessment at six months. The optometrist or pediatric ophthalmologist will test for visual acuity, excessive or unequal amounts of nearsightedness, farsightedness or astigmatism, evaluate eye alignment and examine eye-teaming ability. Of the three to four million babies born every year in the United States, one in 20,000 has retinoblastoma, one in 25 will develop strabismus and one in 30 will develop amblyopia. According to the National

Eye Institute (NEI), an estimated 2.3 million preschool-aged children have an eye disorder that will result in permanent vision loss if not identified and treated.[6-59] Thus, early detection is critical.

Jeffrey Anshel, O.D., states that most visual problems are easier to correct before school age. By grade school, visual disabilities in one area affect learning in other areas, causing a domino effect. If a child has a perceptual delay such as an inability to comprehend spatial relationships, they may not know their left from their right side. They may not know that *g–o* is read as *go* instead of *og*, and they may not see the difference between the letter *b* and the letter *d* — a common pattern seen with children who reverse letters and words. This inability to relate to spatial location can lead to problems in reading, spelling and math.[6-60]

Many visual deficits, if detected in the preschool years, can be resolved with vision training by a developmental optometrist or Natural Vision Practitioner who specializes in vision enhancement for children. Often, if caught in the early stages, the child will completely avoid needing to wear glasses or just wear glasses in the interim to aid in relaxing the visual system while learning, through vision training, to use the eyes in a relaxed way.

Warning Signs of Visual Problems

An eye turning in towards the nose or out is very noticeable, but most parents will not know whether their child has other conditions, such as convergence insufficiency, vergence imbalance, an accommodation problem or visual-perceptual problems. The child will appear to have no symptoms by the parents' observation.

Here is what to observe and/or discuss with your child:
1. Eyes get tired quickly when doing near-point tasks; rubbing eyes
2. Eyestrain; eyes hurt
3. Frequent headaches
4. Squinting
5. Seeing blurry
6. Seeing double
7. Head held up by one arm and turned for only one eye to see paperwork or book to read

With any of these symptoms, get a thorough eye examination for your child that includes testing of near-point visual skills. The American Optometric Association, with The Vision Care Institute of Johnson & Johnson Vision Care, Inc., and former President

Jimmy Carter, have launched InfantSEE™, a national program to provide the pre-school population professional eye and vision care during the early stages. A recent survey revealed that only thirteen percent (13%) of mothers with children younger than 2 years of age had taken their babies to see a vision care professional for a regular check-up. Another astonishing statistic is only fourteen percent (14%) of children younger than the age of six are likely to have had an eye and vision examination.

The InfantSEE™ program provides a no-cost infant eye and vision assessment between the ages of six months and one year. The assessment is recommended to determine if an infant has an identifiable eye or vision condition. Knowing that one in every ten infants is at risk from undiagnosed eye and vision problems may prompt more parents to take advantage of this no-cost program.

Activities to Develop the Sub-Skills of Visual-Perceptual Processing

Some children see 20/20 in the distance, but are their eyes and brain visually equipped to read and to perform other near-point tasks? Are they able to process visual stimuli effectively and efficiently? Visual-perceptual processing can be broken into three components: visual-spatial skills, visual-discrimination skills and visual-integration skills.

The visual-spatial sub-skills are the following:

Laterality: the ability to determine right and left directions on your body

Activities:
- Gallop
- Ride a scooter
- Gorilla walk – Have your child stand with feet together and then bend over to take hold of the ankles. The buttocks are up high and the knees are as straight as possible. "Pick up your left foot and take one gorilla step." "Now pick up your right foot and take one gorilla step." "Now take a few steps on your own." "Now we're ready for a gorilla stroll."

Directionality: the ability to name left/right/up/down in the environment

Activity:
- Flashlight Tag – Each person has a flashlight in a darkened room. One is the leader and the others follow that light. I encourage comfort with being in the dark

by saying, "Let's turn on our night eyes." The child is amazed at how fast the eyes adjust to the darkness and then they actually start to see shapes and forms in the surroundings. Flashlight Tag also enhances eye tracking.

Bilateral Integration: the ability to use the upper and lower parts of the body independently of each other.

Activities:

- Walking a 2" x 4" beam or a rope placed on the floor forward and backward with eyes open and closed. Variation: walk the balance beam with a beanbag on top of the head.

- Standing on a balance board.
  Variations: Two to age 4: bounce a 9-12" rubber ball on the floor while standing on the balance board or throw a beanbag up in the air and catch first with 2 hands and then each hand individually.
  Variations: Five to age 99: bounce racquetballs from each hand simultaneously and alternating (for extensive variations see *Bal-A-Vis-X* videos).[6-61]

- Jumping rope

- Hopping like a rabbit

- Swinging

The visual-discrimination sub-skills and activities to play that develop this skill are as follows:

Figure Ground Discrimination: Can you distinguish a figure (an object) from its background?

Activities:

- "Hocus Focus" in the *Highlights* magazine and "Where's Waldo?"

Visual Form Recognition/Discrimination and Constancy

Activities:

- Tangrams, Parquetry Blocks, Puzzles and the game of *River, Roads and Rails,* which is a fun and cooperative picture-matching game to develop visual discrimination, observational and organizational skills.

Visual Closure

Activities:

- Dot-to-dot and number-to-number pictures

Visual Spatial Memory

Activity:

- Memory Card Games: "Concentration"

Visual Sequential Memory

Activity:

- Start with two or three objects then remove them from view and have the child replicate the sequence. Then increase to four to six objects. It is great to use household objects like a cup, a spoon, dry spaghetti noodles or a dry sponge, or outdoor, natural items like rocks, feathers, leaves, pine cones or acorns from trees.

Visualization

Activities:

- Storytelling; Ask "what would happen" questions, e.g., What would happen if you push the stuffed puppy off the table?

Visual Speed and Span of Perception

Activities:

- "Slap Jack" with playing cards, the game of *Blink*

The Visual Integration Skill

This is the ability to process and integrate visual information, which includes and coordinates input from our other senses and previous experiences so that we can understand what we see. The eye-hand coordination involved in tossing a ball or clapping games like "pat-a-cake" requires a great deal of teamwork between the senses.

Visual-Motor Integration

Twenty percent (20%) of the raw visual data that reaches the retina breaks away from the track to the visual cortex and travels to the brain's motor centers for balance, coordination and movement. Visual-motor integration, commonly called eye-hand or eye-body coordination, is a critical component of vision. The eyes and hands play "follow the leader"– the eyes linked with the mind initiates first and tell the hands where to follow.

Activities:

- Form objects out of clay
- Copy patterns with rubberbands on a Geoboard
- Walk a straight line or Lazy 8 pattern with a paper Victorian butterfly on the index finger
- Have relay races while carrying an object (e.g. small water balloon, egg) on a spoon
- Lacing animals or shoes

- Play *Busy Beetles* never-ending puzzle
- Pick up LEGO® bricks, blocks or other small objects with a wooden tong and move them into a container *Variation*: Give the child the instructions to line up a sequence of colored bricks or blocks that have symbols on them. Start with two items and increase the number as their ability improves.
- Catch marbles rolled one at a time from across the table with a plastic cup. Hold the cup first in one hand for a minute or two and then in the other. The adult varies the direction of rolling the marble to each side, so the child is encouraged to cross the midline with their hand.

Activities to Integrate the Skills of Visual Development

Parents can additionally encourage the following activities to improve the skills of tracking, binocular coordination, fixation, pursuits, depth perception, eye-hand coordination, near-point acuity, far-point acuity and peripheral vision.

Beginning as an infant

- In the first four months, an infant will immediately start to follow moving objects. Talk while you are moving around the room to get their visual and auditory attention.

- Before or after changing diapers, move opposite arm and leg in a Cross Crawl pattern for bilateral and binocular development. Alternate with the other 2 limbs (left arm is moved with the right leg, and the right arm with left leg). Throw in some singing for added pleasure.

- Change the location of the crib in the room and change the position of baby in the crib frequently so the visual stimuli vary.

- Alternate breast-feeding sides not only for lactation purposes but also so baby has a different eye, ear, arm and leg open to the world. The same is true for bottle-feeding.

- Have reach-and-touch toys within baby's range for touching, swatting and kicking. This will be the precursor to depth perception and good eye-hand and eye-foot coordination.

- Play "Peek-a-boo" and "Pat-a-cake"

- Watch for that first time when your baby discovers their right or left hand. It is a magical moment!

For ages 1 and older

- **Ball Rolling** – Sit facing your child with your legs spread wide apart in the shape of a V. As your child gets older you can scoot back further. Both of you take turns rolling 6-12 racquetballs to the other person. One ball at a time. *Variation*: The receiver can count the balls as they come rolling one at a time or call out the colors as they roll towards them. For the wee ones call them out together.

- **Eye Rolls** – Use a finger or a finger puppet, small clicker or stuffed animal (especially the ones that make noise) to have the child watch as you move the object around slowly in a circle in front of their face (clockwise and counterclockwise). As they get older they will be able to do the eye rolls on their own, rotating the eyes around slowly in a big circle 3 times in one direction and then the other, first with eyes open and then with eyes closed. Remind them to breathe and blink during the activity.

- **Marsden Ball** – With a black, fine-point marker put letters randomly all over a 3–4" ball. Next, suspend the ball from the ceiling or a door with a rope or strong string down to the child's eye level. Have the child cover one eye with a patch, push the ball straight forward and then touch one letter each time the ball swings back towards the body's midline. Repeat with the other eye, spending two minutes with each eye monocularly. The purpose of this technique is to develop eye-hand coordination, tracking and fixation skills.

Variations:

- For younger children, use a bigger, softer ball and put symbols instead of letters on the ball.

- Using a dowel or a big wrapping-paper tube as a bunt stick, have the child call out the letters as they tap them. Making a mark at the one-quarter, center and three-quarter points, and calling out right, left or center for the main position of the dowel to use to tap the ball — also develops directionality. Colored tape at those points and calling out red, blue and green would be easier for the wee ones. Putting all three colors on both sides and white in the middle and calling out a combo of a color and a side would be even more challenging.

- Have the child lie down. Slowly swing the ball from side to side in front of their eyes. Then switch to swinging the ball up and down and diagonally. Parent watches for accuracy of child's eye movements in following the swinging ball and encourages the head to be kept still. "What would happen if you kept your head still?"

- Vision tracking (the ability to stay on a visual task)
    - Standing or sitting in front of your child, move a target from side to side in front of their nose. Next, move the target up and down, in and out, diagonally, in circles and in the shape of the infinity sign for one minute. The return swing on the in-and-out is in the path of an arc. When coming straight in to the nose, arc back out and vice versa. Some moving targets to track are a sticker on a tongue depressor, a pen or a finger puppet.
    - Keeping a balloon up in the air using hands, knees, elbows, feet, etc.
    - Blow a bubble and enjoy its colors in the sun.
    - Release a balloon to the sky and watch it disappear
- **Lazy 8s** – in the air, on paper, on the carpet with hands or feet. There are many variations for the Lazy 8s. The focus here is on moving the eyes into all four quadrants of our visual midfield — top, left, bottom and right — while keeping the head still and tracking the Lazy 8 pattern. For a complete description see page 11 in Chapter One.

Finally, with all the hand-held electronic games and computer programs kids play with in this 21st century, it is essential that children be reminded to look to the distance frequently to relax the eyes and to preserve their vision. Encourage them to look and focus at the distance often. The eyes are just not meant to do near-point activity without giving the accommodative eye muscles frequent rest periods. This is a simple habit that in many cases can prevent myopia, commonly known as nearsightedness – a loss of clear distant vision.

The Value of Healthy Visual Development for our Children

Because vision develops so quickly it becomes the major means through which children learn about their world. "Visual development serves as an invaluable guide for understanding every aspect of mental development, including such 'higher' functions as emotions, language and intelligence," states neuroscientist Lise Eliot. Scientists currently know how something as seemingly intangible as visual exposure can permanently change the structure of the brain. The visual experiences and visual-motor activities that children engage in during the early years shape their budding minds.[6-62]

Vision is more than 20/20 eyesight. A child with perfect 20/20 eyesight can still have vision problems, which interfere with their ability to perform at a variety of tasks. Seeing up close and at the distance (near-and far-visual acuity), eye-teaming ability, depth perception, convergence, color vision, tracking and visual-motor integration are all visual abilities that are CRUCIAL for ACADEMIC ACHIEVEMENT to reach one's potential in school as well as in life.

Putting it All Together

Here's a fun activity to develop the auditory, visual, tactile, proprioceptive and vestibular senses mentioned in this chapter. It is also an integrative tool for addressing general categories of movement which, in turn, help to integrate the reflexes.

X Marks The Spot

A traditional rhyme with additional verses and movements by Eve Kodiak.[6-63]

X marks the spot
With a dot and a dot
And a dash and a dash
And a big question mark.
There are upsies and downsies
And downsies and upsies
And pinchies and squeezies
And cool summer breezies.

O goes around
With a pound pound pound pound
And some squiggles and wiggles
And jellyfish jiggles.
There are upsies and downsies
And downsies and upsies
And stripies and wipies
And kitty-cat swipies.

8 makes a gate
Run on in, don't be late
To cut carrots, potatoes
And big red tomatoes.
There are upsies and downsies
And downsies and upsies
And loop-de-loop loops
While we're stirring the soup.

An **8** lying down
And an 8 standing up
Make a clover.
Do it over and over.

These are the specific movements to do on the back of your partner while they are sitting.

X: draw diagonal lines from shoulders to opposite hips

Dot: make a dot between the shoulder blades

And a dot: make a dot at the waist

Dashes: use dot location to make dashes

?: draw over the whole back, dotting at the waist on the word "mark"

Upsies: hands on outsides of back, lightly running up

Downsies: hands on outsides of back, lightly running down

Pinchies and Squeezies: very gently

Cool Summer Breezies: blow toward neck

O: use fist to draw

Pound: gentle pounding with fists

Squiggles, Wiggles, Jiggles: use flats of hands or very light squeeze

Loop: both hands go round as if stirring with a ladle

8: draw a "lazy 8" across shoulder blades

Run on in: use two fingers to run across the back

Cut: sides of hands, chopping gently

Stripies, Wipies, Swipies: gentle "claws" moving diagonally across back

Clover (8 lying down and standing up): draw a lazy eight. When you return to the middle, draw an upright 8. Repeat "over and over."

According to Eve Kodiak, musician and licensed Brain Gym® consultant, "playing **X Marks the Spot** requires one to use all of the reflex categories: Whole Body Breathing (coordinating speaking and rhythm, and especially the 'cool summer breezies'), Navel Radiation (stroking the back helps to define and integrate the core), Mouthing (coordinating speaking with hand movements), Spinal (activating the spine through touch, also 'pound' and 'squiggles and wiggles and jellyfish jiggles'), Homologous ('upsies and downsies'), homolateral ('dot' and 'dash'), contralateral (just about everything!) and, of course, cross-lateral ('X Marks the Spot'). As with all integrating movement activities, **X Marks the Spot** works both ways. Playing it helps to integrate reflexes. And doing specific reflex movements helps the student to achieve the rhythm and dexterity to do **X Marks the Spot**."

▲ **Puppy pileup**

A child is a whole being. Their vision, hearing, proprioception, touch, taste, smell and the vestibular system are all related in subtle and sometimes obvious ways. Any impairment results in surprising and deep deficits in perception and action. Academic skills, such as reading, require very complex sensory integration from the eyes, the inner ears, and the eye and neck muscles. Many play activities like turning, rolling, jumping, climbing, bending and pushing produce a tremendous amount of tactile, visual, auditory, proprioceptive and vestibular input.[6-64] Sometimes the most fun and beneficial activity to do with your family is to playfully pile on top of each other like a bunch of puppies, laughing and giggling and enjoying the sensations.

The sensory integration that occurs in talking, moving and playing is the groundwork for reading and all cognitive functions.

If sensory-motor functions are well organized before kindergarten, a child will have an easier time learning all academics in school.[6-65]

Guiding your
child's spirit

Do your eyes light up when your child comes into the room?

Nurturing Moment

Before pre-school one day when my son Kevin was five years old, he complained that he was not feeling well. He was scheduled to go on a field trip that day and I sensed he was feeling apprehensive about the outing. Then he said, "I wish my school didn't have field trips." This confirmed my suspicion. Rather than go into all the great reasons a parent knows that field trips are good for kids, I took the opportunity while he was putting on his shoes and tying his shoelaces to hold his Positive Points (a Brain Gym activity). This was accomplished by placing my fingers halfway between the hairline and the eyebrows. The hands are held with the three middle fingers positioned vertically. The spot is directly in line with the pupils of the eyes when looking straight ahead.

After that moment of pause, Kevin went off to play and he never made mention again about feeling sick or not wanting to go on the field trip. It is so important to hold the space for the child to feel their feelings. This simple Brain Gym activity calmed the "butterflies" by connecting to the frontalis muscle and the neurovascular points for the stomach meridian, which improves the blood circulation to the stomach.[7-1] When the frontalis muscle is relaxed, one can feel the normal pulse of blood going into the foramen under the fingers, providing nerves and blood to the frontal sinuses and the brain.[7-2] Positive Points also activated the frontal lobes of the brain so Kevin was able to think about the outing from a new perspective.

Laura Belle Wynne, a Spiritual Counselor in Sedona, Arizona, declares: "Parents, listen to your children. They came back with the wisdom. Children today are extremely advanced souls. They are bored to tears with parents repeating over and over again the same things. This drives the child crazy."[7-3] So many old belief systems are passed down from generation to generation that no longer apply. For example, why do we need to have three square meals a day? Who started that rule? Why were we told to finish eating all the food on our plate? Who's starving where? So much food gives children a tummy ache due to their inability to digest big portions all at once. Kids have a small stomach. Have them make a fist and you'll see how big it is. Why force them to eat when their brain tells them they are full? We want them to notice for themselves when they are getting the message from their brain that they are finished eating.

Healthy Lifestyle Choice

Eating for Nourishment to Live

Food is a big issue in some families today. How the early years are experienced subconsciously create the foundation for a lifetime of eating habits. There are two lifestyle choices:

• *Eating for nourishment to live* (healthy choice)

• *Emotional living to eat ...*
The second choice leads to obesity and eating disorders such as bulimia and anorexia. With frequent big meals and lack of daily physical exercise, our children are becoming overweight and, worse yet, obese. Let's empower them to act on their knowingness and stop when they are full instead of eating everything on their plate to fill a void or to please us. If you don't want to waste food, serving smaller portions is an option. We all have a choice in taking seconds and there are health benefits in grazing throughout the day with high-nutrient laden foods!

Avoid giving children food when they are upset. As parents, we never want to see our children hurting emotionally or physically. Out of our own distress with the hurt our child may be experiencing, many of us act to make them feel better immediately. Rather than letting them process their feelings of sadness, frustration, anger, fear or pain in the moment, some parents give a piece of candy, a cookie or a bowl of ice cream to distract them. Then the child makes the association that sweets make them better, rather than learning that feeling their feelings will naturally help them through their discomfort. It is very empowering to experience the skill of self-comforting.

The desire for sweets can become a craving. World-renowned heart surgeon Dr. Mehmet Oz explains how some cravings are physical and others have an emotional origin. The mammillary bodies near the hypothalamus, receiving a major bundle of hippocampal fibers, control both memory and cravings. How are these two functions intertwined? According to Dr. Oz, when you're two years old and you're having a bad time and your mother gives you a fatty food, this part of your brain remembers that. Right next door, when the satiety center says to eat food, the place it draws its memory from, is right next to it. So the mammillary bodies say, "The last time you had that cream pudding, it took care of your problem." The reason you can be stopped dead in your tracks by the smell of cookies baking is because that smell registers right in the middle of your brain. Dr. Oz states, "It bypasses your thought process, it's a reflex. It mainlines right into the middle of your brain and you don't have any ability to control that."[7-4]

▲ **Mother holding daughter's Positive Points.**

Pausing Moment Activities For Those Upset Times

Here are a few "Pausing Moment" activities so children can learn to calm or even, in some situations, heal themselves: A child can (1) hold their own Positive Points (as described above) or (2) get into Hook-Ups (as described in Chapter 3) and another person can hold the child's Positive Points or (3) do the Ouchy Clearing. Instruct them to "concentrate your energy inside your body and head, breathing to the places of pain or discomfort." Vary the wording with a very young child: "Breathe to those yucky places inside that are ouching to you." I never used words like "headache" with my son when he was very young. I never said, "Do you have a headache?" I believed if we could clear the pain without attaching words to it, he would stay healthier and happier. He was six or seven when he had his first headache and told me, "My brain hurts." I had to laugh at how cute that sounded.

If a child is able to speak, say "Can you locate it in your body? How big is it? Does it have a color? Does it have a texture? If it could talk, what would it say?" Let them talk about the feeling, whether physical or emotional. Some children are too young to express what they are feeling in words and others have a hard time verbalizing when they are hurt or emotional, so for them just start by saying, "Touch those ouchy places."

Pausing

• Positive Points
• Hook-Ups
• Ouchy Clearing

When my son was very young I would use gibberish to help him voice his feelings. If he hit a table by accident or a ball hit him, I would start talking gibberish to the table or ball and throw in Kevin's name and the object's name amongst the gibberish. This made him laugh and then the pain went away. He has fond memories of those gibberish moments.

Let's not teach our children to run to food or to a chemical pain reliever when they have a pain. This may lead to chronic use of drugs and/or alcohol as an adult in order to cope with or, worse yet, numb the feelings. Sometimes just cuddling with your child is all that is needed. Do we want to be remembered for always cleaning the house, talking on the phone or being on the computer, or do we want our children to remember us spending quality moments with our loved ones? There is nothing more important than letting our children know by our actions that they are special to us and they are the most important people in our life. If we don't take the time with our children, who will?

Our children know much more than we realize. Laura Belle Wynne asserts, "Parents must listen to their children and also find out how to be with them so you can have joy and peace in the home. We are living in a new world. The Energy on the planet has changed. It is a new planet. This is a dawning of a new day, a new

▲ **Daddy's cuddle time with his sons.**

world, a new era. All teaching has to be done on a new level. Parents must learn what they must do to change their old ways."[7-5]

We are preparing our children to excel in school and grow into self-sufficient, successful adults. They are very capable of doing many things if we take the time to teach them every step of the way. It will pay off immensely in the long run. Let them figure things out for themselves with your guidance and supervision. Start early with this one.

How many times have you heard, "Mom, what's a _____ ?" "Miss Jones, what's that for?" "Dad, but why?" "Mom, how do you spell _____?" No matter what age (and it starts very early) the only difference is that as they get older, the questions get more difficult to answer and the words get harder to spell. My mother would respond astutely when we were young with the same answer, "Look it up." English was a second language for her so she didn't want to give us the wrong information and, more importantly, she wanted us to learn how to find things out for ourselves.

Of course with little ones, they are too young to look it up, but you can start your discussion with "What do you think, _____?" Watch their active imagination create and then you can add to that with a bit of what you know. Active involvement by parents and other caring adults sends the message that we care and we want to empower our children to "Be the Best You that You can Be." When my son asks me how to spell a certain word, my response is, "What do you think?" He gets it right 99% of the time! We need to stop and pause a moment so they have the space to retrieve the answer from their brilliant mind.

> "Listen to your children when they are speaking. Many children feel that no one listens to them! Some challenged children are hyper and have a hard time listening; and they also feel that they are not heard. When they experience slowing down and hearing, and also being heard, they 'get it' and life truly transforms! I see this all the time! I might add that this is for EVERYONE. This is about honoring yourself and others as we are all connected in this Universe!"
>
> – Jeanne Belli, RN, Cranio Sacral Therapist, Clinical Hypnotherapist, Massage Therapist, and Brain Gym Consultant

Laura Belle Wynne says, "Parents get wise. The old world, the old teachings are dead and gone. Our children can't stand it any more— the lecturing, the 'do it because I say so.' They live by the TV and the Net. Parents are losing all control."[7-6]

I have heard parents lose control and yell to their child, "What's wrong with You?" or "What's the matter with You?" when the child is hitting or accidentally spills their glass of milk or won't stop whining. It is very tempting to label them with a deficiency or defect. The hidden message the child gets is that there must be something Very Wrong with ME. They may start feeling that they can never do anything right and nothing is ever good enough. When heard over and over again, they begin to believe that there is definitely something wrong with them and their Self-Esteem suffers. It then starts affecting their daily activities and when they enter school, they have already established a failure syndrome. "I can't do anything right." "I'm no good at that." A big part of their energy goes to this negative conversation inside their head instead of being 100% present for learning.

Have realistic expectations for your children. Remember their young, inexperienced age. Remember none of us were born with a brain that could do anything and everything from day one. We all, as infants and children, grew our brain and created neuro-pathways through moving and doing.

Encouragement

Encouragement supports children to be their very best and feel whole. Genuine encouragement goes a long way in building self-confidence, self-esteem and intelligence. In addition, it helps kids know they are on the right track with their performance and behavior. If a child is misbehaving, take a look at whether they feel discouraged and lack a sense of belonging. Have faith in your child and their ability to develop skills. Point out their strengths and how their actions make you feel. "That really makes me smile! I see it makes you smile, too." Let's not discourage them with words of criticism, judgment, inadequacy and fear. It takes courage to do something new. I found that when my son and I did a task together the first few times, his self-confidence would build to the point that he was willing to take the initiative on his own. Most subconscious messages have been implanted in the mind by age six. So how wonderful it would be to have a positive self-image of success instilled from the early beginnings!

"What would happen if ___?" is a lead-in phrase to guide a child into new possibilities without demanding them to do it your way or discouraging them all together with a "You're too young" comment. For example, you are packing for a trip and your three or four-year-old daughter or son wants to pack their own clothes. You notice them balling the shirts, pants and shorts up and stuffing them in the suitcase. To encourage the

33 Ways to Encourage a Child

- That's Amazing to Me!
- I Know You'll Do Your Best!
- Go For It!
- Wow!
- You're Catching On!
- That Was Courageous!
- I'm Glad You Enjoy ____!
  e.g., I'm Glad You Enjoy Brushing Your Teeth!
- I Appreciate What You Have Done!
- Take All the Time You Need!
- Give It a Whirl!
- Well Done!
- The Beginning Really Has Me Intrigued! I Can Hardly Wait To See How You Decide To Finish It!
- You're On Top Of It!
- I Really Like How It Turned Out!
- You're A Real Trooper!
- You Go, Girl! or You Go, Boy!

- How Clever!
- I Like It When _____!
  e.g., I Like It When You Use All Those Colors!
- What A Unique Way To Do That!
- Great Discovery!
- You Figured It Out!
- I'm Glad You Can Do It!
- Now You've Got It!
- You're On Your Way!
- My Favorite Part Of Your _____ Is/Was_____. What Is Your Favorite Part?
- Nothing Can Stop You Now!
- You're Growing Up!
- I'm Proud Of You!
- Beautiful Work!
- Creative Job!
- I Trust You'll Figure It Out!
- Way To Go!
- What An Imagination!

act, you might say, " I am so happy to see you packing your own clothes for the trip. What a big girl/boy thing to do. What would happen if the pants were folded here first and then rolled?" You haven't discouraged their willingness to contribute and you have gently suggested a different approach. Any attempt on their part deserves acknowledgement of their accomplishment. So what if the clothes are folded a little crooked? I was always thrilled at my son's willingness to participate.

Other forms of positive reinforcement and encouragement are a big smile, honoring eye contact, appropriate touch, a big kiss, a thumbs-up, a High-Five, a High-X-Ten (you and the child cross your own arms to make an X and then clap the other person's hands) and the most physically and emotionally balancing of all, a Heart-to-Heart hug.

Pausing Moment Activity To Raise Self-Esteem

Another way to raise the self-esteem of a child is by making a special note that they can hang on the refrigerator or in their bedroom.

Let your child know in your own words how special they are to you and how much your eyes light up when they walk into the room. Fold the paper and write their name in cursive on the outside and decorate it artistically to show them what they are to you in art form: suns, hearts, waves, trees, etc. Draw whatever comes to mind when you think of this child. Then sit in one of those "pause moments" and read the letter with them. Have them put their name in a variety of colors that they choose all around

Taylor

Taylor

Taylor

Taylor

Dear Taylor,

You are Lovable!
You are Special to Me!
You are a Treasure!
You are Sweetness and Light!
You are Imaginative!
You are Incredible!
You are Wonderful!
You are dancing in Life!
Being around You Brightens my day!

I Love You!   Dad xxx ooo

the writing of your letter. (Centering the note in the middle of the paper allows room for them to write their name surrounding it.) A child writing their name over and over has a very profound, positive effect on their self-esteem.

For those who are very young and don't know their letters, they can put their first letter or any scribble that is how they think their name might look. Make a big deal of any attempt to do it. If a letter is reversed, who cares It is not about being perfect; it is about being in the process and feeling good about the creation.

Notice that I purposely did not include things that she can DO, like "You are a great piano player!" or "You are athletic!" or "You read well!" I want her to know I love her, regardless of her strengths or weaknesses. Kids need to know we, as caring adults, will love them no matter what, even when we experience them as cranky or misbehaving. We may not like their behavior in a particular moment, but we do not love them any less. We do not need to bribe them with food or money to behave. Our love is not conditional. Sitting still and "Being Nice" are not requirements for our affection and attention.

A Nurturing Moment

Feelings are feelings. They are not right or wrong. Sometimes they just need to be expressed in a safe environment where no one will make the child feel wrong for having them. Here's a fascinating example of how feelings can be transformed when we hold the space for them to be okay!

A five-year-old boy named A.G. was being really defiant and uncooperative at a private session with me one day. He didn't want to do any Brain Gym. He was exhibiting so much resistance. Even after I had calmly told him to stop throwing the balls and Frisbee aggressively, he continued ignoring me. "What are you angry about?" I asked. He opened up to explain that he was upset that I didn't have the usual rocker he likes out and available for him. We did some activities to integrate the Joy reflex. They were very difficult for him to do and he was complaining how it was so hard and hurt.

Then he told me how much he hated me. I stayed in my heart-space because I really wanted him to move through all the anger. I said, "Yes, sometimes my son says he hates me, too." I gave him permission for his feelings. I chose not to make him wrong for sounding mean. I didn't try to convince him to feel otherwise or lecture him on why it's bad to hate someone. He shared his feelings and then was ready to move on.

Next he told me how much he hated Brain Gym and he wasn't coming back. So I pulled out an 8 ½ X 11 piece of paper and had him put all his hate on the paper scribbling with a crayon. Well, it got so big and overflowing that I pulled out a big piece of paper. (Moving paper works great! They sell it by the box at moving companies.) I next said, "Okay, now let's do it with both hands because I know there is more hate that can come out through your other hand, too!" Well, he ended up filling the big paper with double doodles. I wasn't about to tell him that he just did a Brain Gym activity called The Double Doodle. It sure was fun to watch him expressing himself with his hands.[7-7]

It was very interesting to observe that the big crayons worked better because he could hold the crayons with a power grip that looks like a fist. He had both those fists moving all over the paper and very fast! By the end he flipped the paper over and showed me with a blue crayon, and by his own impetus, how much he hated Brain Gym and he also wanted me to know how much he liked Brain Gym.

The size of the hate had shrunk to the size of a dime and the size of how much he liked Brain Gym was about the size of a dinner plate and in bright yellow like the sun. Wow, what a beautiful process! I was so thrilled and happy that he felt safe enough around me to share his feelings. He even chose to hug me when saying Good-bye!

Respect

We have had too many generations of children "being seen and not heard." It is no wonder they feel a strong urge to rebel by the time they are teenagers. Children need to be respected from birth— well, actually from conception but that is a whole other book. Webster's Dictionary defines respect as "to take notice of; to regard with special attention; to regard as worthy of special consideration; to consider worthy of esteem; to regard with honor."

Let your children know that

- They make a difference in your world
- Their thoughts matter
- Keeping them safe is your intention
- They are a treasure in your life
- What they say is important to you
- They are worthy of all the magic and wonder the world has to offer, and above all
- Their very Existence matters.

When they are safe, secure and feel whole, life is an adventure. They wake up looking forward to having a great day. Even learning becomes one of life's most exciting games! The other day I was cleaning the house and found a note that my son (age 9) had written on an index card.

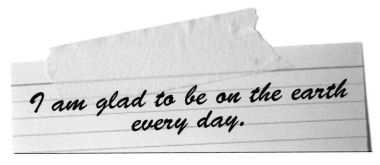

I am glad to be on the earth every day.

Don't we want all kids feeling this way?

We teach best by example— model to them how to be respectful by being respectful to others, including children. I am always so grateful when my son has a respectful teacher. It makes a big difference in the tone of the class and creates a mentally healthy atmosphere for learning.

What kind of model are we for our children? If we are their caregiver, teacher or therapist, it may be easier to have more patience. After all, we are being paid. As a parent, our reactions sometimes are different. Parenting can bring up all sorts of "old-baggage" stuff. When you see and experience cruelty and/or abandonment as a child, that is what you know. In your own innocent world, you think all parents treat their children that way. It would be so natural to fall into that pattern unconsciously as an adult. Here is our opportunity today to consciously choose how we are in each moment with our loved ones. If we find ourselves in a power play, notice the reaction coming into the body and pause to take a deep breath (or two or three) to chemically and neurologically change the reaction to a heart-centered response.

One of my husband's friends, S.E.W., was visiting with his seven-year-old twins one weekend and I marveled at how respectful he was with them. I was curious to know what he thought being respectful of your children meant. He said, "Parents, part of respect is to listen to your children and be aware of their thoughts, moods, behaviors and desires. As parents we are all caught up with ourselves and end up making the kids do what we want them to do. We get distracted. We don't hear what they say."

It happens to all of us and we can choose to become conscious and stop in that moment, take a deep breath and let them know (1) "I really want to hear what you just said, so please repeat it." Or, if our distracting task absolutely cannot wait, (2) say "I can't process what you are saying now, and I really want to hear it in just a minute." They need to know that they are not a bother to us. They will also be learning to develop patience and delayed gratification for themselves. As for the wee little ones, a simple "Say it again!" while honestly listening will suffice.

It is important to respect boundaries and feelings. Boundaries are a two-way street. We want to set boundaries for children so they are secure in their world and we want them to establish their own boundaries so they will speak up for themselves when they know peers or adults have crossed the line. NO means NO and that goes both ways. When someone is tickling a child, there is a fine line between pleasure and pain. The child needs to know when he or she exclaims "Stop!" the tickler will stop immediately. If you don't, you have invaded their boundaries, their safe space and your bond of trust has been jeopardized. Why should they respect the boundaries you set for them with those mixed messages? Let us be clear and follow through with our word. The old proverb still rings true: "Actions speak louder than words."

According to the Father of Psychoanalysis, Sigmund Freud, "The key to the successful adjustment in each stage is how well parents help their child adjust to the stage and make the transition to the next stage." The challenge lies in maintaining a balance between the extremes. Parents must be conscious that they are not displaying perfectionistic or over-protective tendencies nor, at the other extreme, a lack of caring.[7-7]

How We Speak — Communication

We can manifest respect through our communication. How we speak to children affects their physiology. The tone of our voice, the words we choose, eye contact and body language are extremely impactful. Some communication causes stress to their young bodies and emotional psyche, and others are empowering. Young children are particularly sensitive to the tone of people's voices. Thirty-eight percent of communication is transmitted by the tone of the voice.

Our choice of words makes a difference. When we tell a child to "try harder," they lose whole-brain function. Most of their energy is directed to the effort of completing the task and the mind chatter of reoccurring thoughts rather than relaxing and enjoying the process. We can support children by encouraging them to "do their best." They need to hear what we want them to do, not what they shouldn't do. If a child is climbing up high because that is what young kids naturally do, it is better to say in a calm tone, "Move steady," or " Be Careful," instead of "Watch out that you don't Fall!" or "Don't Fall!" or "You're going to Fall!" for the young child's brain resonates with the word "Fall" and they often fulfill your fear.

Let's look at the term "Terrible Twos." Who programmed that one to be so bad? If you plan for the Terrible Twos, that is exactly what you will see in your child. This principle has been repeated over and over with quantum physics. What you expect and look for is what you will receive and live. I have heard mothers at the park say, "Oh she's in her Terrible Twos stage." That is a sure-fire order for a day filled with tantrums. Your thoughts, words and vibrational energy are the recipe for the day ahead. We feed off each other's energy. Fortunately, we have the power to make the change in an instant. Tapping is a simple way to reprogram yourself. While tapping the "Karate" point on the side of the hand below the baby finger with the fingertips of the other hand, say out loud, " Even though I have this ____, I deeply and completely love and accept myself." For example, "Even though I have this feeling of frustration now, I deeply and completely love and accept myself." When a parent shifts to inner peace, acceptance and knowingness even in the midst of chaos, the child senses safety and security. The calmer the parent can focus on being, the calmer the child shall be. When a toddler turns two, it would be wonderful to have a celebration of the Terrific Twos. Let's start a new tradition and make the Terrible Twos a thing of the past!

A Nurturing Moment Story:

One evening when Kevin was 6 years old, I was feeling upset with his behavior because he kept playing when it was time for bed. After a while he called me to come to his room and kiss him good night. He said with a wise tone in his voice, "We can be upset but we always love each other."

As a caring adult, you may want to reconsider parental upbringing, relationships and teaching styles to assist your children in avoiding needless frustration, achieving balance and finding harmony in their lives. Let's give our children respect, validation and discipline, and recognize that our role as "parent" is to understand the beauty of the higher level of consciousness in today's children for the new society that is evolving. Expect the best from your children and celebrate the accomplishments whether big or small!

Now pause a moment and connect with a child.

Favorite connecting
activities

"Play is the only way the highest intelligence of humankind can unfold."

— Joseph Chilton Pearce

I recently queried a network of people around the world about their favorite activity to do with their children, students and clients. I thought it might be interesting to read about other peoples' approach in connecting with our future leaders.

Prenatal (as a pregnant Momma)

"I have so many favorite moments with my son, Court, that it's hard to pick just one. He has always been his own person with a desire to protect others. He has had a mind of his own and has never been afraid to express his opinion. Even before he was born he would let his opinions be known. His kicks would remind me that a pregnant woman needs to take a break when moving a woodpile long before I was aware that I should take a break."

– Jan Hunt, remembering
moments with son Court

Birth to Age Two (as a Parent)

"Hug your child and smile at her or him."

– Isabelle Fernandez

"Crawling games with contrast toys. Talking with her. 'Peek-a-boo' type games and 'So big.' Stroller rides and walks through parks, Sea World® and the beach, naming everything. Finger painting and sidewalk chalk (had I known Lazy Eights then!!!) Songs and dance. Rolling a large ball back and forth. Reading big storybooks, fabric storybooks, and pop-up books everyday."

– June Heinz

"Sing and dance/move to music."

– Nadine Iba

"I loved breastfeeding and bonding with my babies. I also did a lot of singing of children's songs with them and they did their best to sing along."

– Patricia Rendon

"Rhymes and songs, many with actions which we incorporate into almost every aspect of Feigie's life; Brain Gym to songs; massage; we also love reading and playing in the park on the see-saw, swings, slide and playing with balls, and generally enjoying nature and movement and water play with bubble fun."

– Marcelle Goldsmith Shaman

Age One (as a Parent)

"Oats in a bowl – This idea was given to me when my children were about a year old. You place a cup of dry rolled-oats in a bowl and give them a wooden spoon. The whole idea is that they are helping mommy cook. What is great about the oats is that if it spills over onto the floor it actually attracts dust so when you sweep it up you are cleaning your floor also."

– Wendy Retzer

Age Two to Four (as a Parent)

"Play 'pretend' with her, and see what ideas she comes up with."

– Isabelle Fernandez

"Reading and moving to music of their choosing."

– Nadine Iba

"Continuing with the activities that she enjoyed before turning two, especially storybooks (see June Heinz above-Birth to Age Two) plus a ITTYL Phonics program that was superb. We added bike riding, swimming lessons at swim school (very sweet and gentle). I let her guide me in what interested her. Throw and catch, and kickball. Rhyming and word games. Make up stories. Sharlyn dictated an incredible unicorn story at age four. Coloring and drawing were her favorites. Hunts, à la Easter eggs, all year round! We always hit educational and craft stores. We spent lots of time exploring at Balboa Park, San Diego Zoo®, Sea World®, watching movies and some traveling."

– June Heinz

"We danced and they played a lot of imaginative games together. They socialized a lot with the neighborhood children, and loved to jump and hop. Again, singing was a big thing for us."

– Patricia Rendon

"Here's an idea for painting: choose non-toxic paints. Have the children in their diapers, underpants or swimsuits. They can take paintbrushes or their hands and paint all over the bathtub walls and door. Also, this activity can be modified to have the children paint the sliding glass door if people have one in their homes.

Another fun paint activity is to take one cardboard box, a large piece of paper that fits in the bottom of the box, and some marbles and paint. Squirt several different colors of paint on the paper at the bottom of the box; place the marble on the paper and paint, then have the kids move the box all around, making the marbles roll all over the paper. It will be a very unique design when you take it out to dry."

– Wendy Retzer

"A Sandbox idea for Rainy Days: purchase an under-the-bed box or find something similar in size around your home. Go to any home improvement store and buy a bag of sand. Place the sand in the box. Put a large picnic table cloth down on the ground then place the box on top of that in your kitchen. The children had a great time playing in the sand while I made dinner. This box could be placed in the garage or anywhere in the house where it would be quite easy to vacuum up the sand."

– Wendy Retzer

Age Four to Six (as a Parent)

"I talk to her about things she doesn't know and see what she says about them and the questions she asks."

– Isabelle Fernandez

"Reading and game-playing, and also dancing and moving to music."

– Nadine Iba

"We continued to do the same activities as during the early years, and they started to learn to ride a tricycle and bicycle at that age. We played 'ring around the rosy'-type games in Spanish. (Our daughters lived with us in Colombia until ages 5 and 7.)"

– Patricia Rendon

"Sharlyn was a fluent reader at the time, so we read A LOT! We did a lot of writing and she could read and spell before kindergarten...again, hard on visual processing, I fear! She continued swimming, scootering, bicycling (not her favorite) and roller blading. Lots of museums, zoos, restaurants and such. She started piano lessons at six and she still plays with the same instructor; very mellow and nurturing. Because Sharlyn has a tendency to be very creative and check out, we used lots of early learning, big movement strategies. But alas I didn't know Brain Gym yet.

She did some OT activities with me like trampoline work. She did some LEGO and block work, but was always more drawn to art. She began soccer, but only played three years, from 6-9."

– June Heinz

Stories

"My daughter, Melanie, just turned 4. Everyone tells me that she is very awake and surprising in her thoughts. I don't know, I only have one child, but she is definitely very interesting to talk to and to listen to. For instance, when Melanie was two-and-a-half we went to Europe to see the family. We had to take two planes which she loved in spite of the 14 hours of flying, and when we got back home, she always wanted to play and pretend we were going back there, preparing the luggage, going to the airport,

taking the plane and arriving at my parents. That was taking
all her toy bags, suitcases, doll stroller and dolls, sitting on the
couch, attaching our seatbelts and leaving the couch with all her
stuff again to go ring at the grandparents."

– Isabelle Fernandez

"One of my favorite moments with my son happened when I
was helping at his Special Education preschool. His teacher ran
in from the playground to have me witness a moment that I will
never forget. Five-
year-old Court was
standing chest-high
to a sixth-grade bully.
As I listened closely, I
wanted to cheer him
on, but he didn't need
any help.

Court was
protecting his little
friend. His friend
had been born with a
rare syndrome. The boy was undergoing surgery after surgery
to build eyelids, a nose and ears. The sixth grade boys were
pointing and laughing at Court's little friend. The biggest boy
laughed as he pointed and scoffed, 'What happened to him?'

Court stepped closer to the bully and calmly explained, 'You
were born with brown hair and brown eyes. This is how my
friend was born.' Court took his little friend by the hand and said,
'Let's go play.' The bullies just stood there, dumbfounded."

– Jan Hunt

"I was used to receiving calls from my son's teachers
complaining about his inability to pay attention in class. In the
first grade, I received a call from his teacher complaining that
my son, Court, never paid attention when she was talking to the
class. When he came home from school, I asked him what he was
doing while his teacher was talking to the class. He said that he
had found a boy on the other side of the room who knew how to
throw 'mind color balls.' They were literally playing ball while the
teacher was conducting a lesson.

Court was very open about any subject at that age. Nobody in
his family judged him and he felt safe. It was not until later in life
that he learned about discernment, and that there were certain
people to whom you could tell certain things and other people

who were best to avoid telling secrets. I asked Court if he could teach me how to play 'mind color balls.' He looked at me in a quizzical way and asked, 'Don't you know how to play mind color balls?'

He explained, 'Mom, just think of a colored ball and think it to me. I'll catch it in my mind and tell you what color it is. Then I'll think you a colored ball.' After a few practice balls, and a lot of patience from Court, we were playing 'mind color ball.' Court complimented me with, 'See, Mom. You can do it. The mind is a power tool.' I clarified, 'A *powerful* tool?' He replied, 'Whatever you want to call it, Mom. Just don't forget to use all of your mind. At school, we only get to use the boring part, and not the fun part.'

From then on, instead of taking the furniture apart in a waiting room, or complaining about waiting for a doctor, all I had to do was ask Court to play, 'mind color ball.' Sometime in our childhood, we forget to use our entire mind and need a child to switch on the 'power tool'."

– Jan Hunt

Activities with Clients

The following activities have been used with clients and as you will discover, they are also fun for parents too.

Infants to age Two with Clients

"With infants: I am touching and listening to their body — what are they saying. I use cranio-sacral therapy and am aligned with the energy and listening and being one in love."

– Jeanne Belli, RN, Cranio-Sacral Therapist, Clinical Hypnotherapist,
Massage Therapist and Brain Gym Consultant

"Brain Gym to music both singing and recorded. Playing on the large ball (about beach-ball size), rolling forward and backward and sideways and in a circle, walking forward on his/her hands to pick up an object, and sitting and bouncing on the ball incorporating rhymes and song."

– Marcelle Goldsmith Shaman, mother and Occupational
Therapist/Brain Gym practitioner, co-author of Hands On:
How to use Brain Gym® in the Classroom

Eight Months to Two Years with Clients

Infant Obstacle Course

By Jon Bredal, MA, Educational Consultant

1. Create an obstacle course with pillows, cushions, chairs, a large ball, etc.

2. Encourage your baby to move through the course by modeling for her how to move.

3. Place a toy on a large pillow so your baby is motivated to crawl up on the pillow to get the toy. Then place the toy on the floor for her to retrieve.

4. Build a tunnel for your baby to crawl through by placing a blanket over 2-3 chairs.

5. Place different textures on the floor for your baby to move over.

6. Give your baby the opportunity to move on a slick surface to improve balance.

7. Place a large ball in front of your baby and help her to move on top of it. Then rock her gently back and forth.

8. Slide her down the ball so she can kick off with her feet and push off with her hands.

9. Create a surface with a slope so she can crawl up and down the surface.

10. Encourage your baby to crawl over your body as part of the obstacle course.

Age Two to Four with Clients

"Using Brain Gym, I begin with guided Cross Crawls while they lie on their backs. Jumbo Lazy 8s at the beach in wet sand and also on the sidewalk with chalk. Bean bag tossing, throw and catch. Skipping and song and dance. Rhyming games. Hunts, looking for one object...then remembering up to three objects to hunt for in a small room. I call this 'executive function training' and I do it with older kids who need it. Find these things and organize them for your day... great as a pre-activity with a balance...progressing in difficulty for older kids."

– June Heinz, Director of the Abilities
Family Learning Center/Academic Coach

▲ "With the child on a ball about the size of a beach ball, I add more complexity than with infant to two-year-olds. For example, picking up a bean bag while lying on tummy on a ball and throwing it at a target across the midline; Brain Gym to music and on equipment, e.g., jumping on a trampoline, standing on a wobbly board for balance and incorporating stories."

– Marcelle Goldsmith Shaman

Now It's Time

By Jon Bredal, MA, Educational Consultant

Sit on the floor with your children and sing the following song to the tune of "*London Bridge*" and do the actions:

Now it's time to <u>lie on our stomach</u>
<u>Lie on our stomach</u>, <u>lie on our stomach</u>
Now it's time to <u>lie on our stomach</u>
My fair children.

Now it's time to <u>look around</u> ... (resting on forearms)

Now it's time to <u>roll side-to-side</u> ... (roll with arms overhead starting from both back and stomach)

Now it's time to <u>crawl on our belly</u> ... (pushing off from knee and reaching out with opposite arm)

Raise right up ... *(arms straight under shoulders supporting whole body)*

Get up on all fours ... *(in a four-point crawling position and look around)*

Rock our body ... *(small rocking movements from front to back)* ▶

Sit like a cat ... *(move our head on the floor)*

Move our head on the floor ... *(top of head moves on floor supported by hands on the floor)*

Move back and forth ... *(from cat-sit position looking up and then hands on floor with head down)*

Move our head up and down ... *(look down at floor and up at ceiling)*

Move our head side-to-side ... *(move head from side-to-side)*

Crawl around ... *(on all fours look all around)*

Spin in circles ... *(spin on knees, stomach or on bottom)*

Walk like a robot ... *(very stiff with slight pause in between each movement)*

Walk like a human ... *(with style)*

This playful activity takes children through basic developmental movement patterns.

Age Four to Six with Clients

"As a school counselor, my main work is in schools in regular ed., so I do a lot of PACE with my kinder students and use water and Hook-ups to calm those children who have separation anxiety."

– Patricia Rendon, Professional School Counselor

"I am a kinesiologist, and my favorite activity to do with children aged 4 to 6 is to allow them to choose a brush from the collection I have, or to bring one of their own for body brushing, also called dry brushing. Baby brushes, mushroom or vegetable brushes, even toothbrushes work well.

I learn about the child's sensory system needs by asking the child if they would like their feet, arms, legs or face brushed. If a child really likes 'brushing,' then I know that the amount of sensory information that most people are okay with is too much stimulation for this child. Some children feel bombarded by the information collected through the senses because the brain can't separate stimulation that is meaningful in terms of survival from the feel of the tag inside a shirt. All stimulation is perceived as important, and this is overwhelming. It puts them on alert.

'Brushing' of large areas of skin (like arms and legs) overcomes the part of the brain that analyzes sensory information. The result is that the Reticular Activating System (RAS) can discern important stimuli from non-threatening stimuli. The result is a child who is more focused and less anxious.

"Some children wiggle, giggle or smile and purr when they are 'brushed.' Most often after a good 'brushing' children are calm and flexible in temperament. They like it so much they do it on their own, and teach their parent what they like as well."

– Tina Baker, Kinesiologist

"My favorite activity with young children is PLAYING — playing and connecting in conversation while sitting on a ball."

– Jeanne Belli, RN, Cranio-Sacral Therapist,
Clinical Hypnotherapist, Massage Therapist and Brain Gym Consultant

"I love big writing for four- and five-year-olds in wet sand, and with sidewalk chalk and shaving cream. Playing musical instruments while saying multisyllable words for reading fluency, like pounding a drum or shaking a tambourine to each beat of 'mo/men/tar/i/ly.' Brain Gym's Alphabet 8s and alphabet writing on a big board. When parents and schools allow, I move into cursive when the student demonstrates readiness, long before they teach it in school. This can really help students with learning issues avoid years of frustrations. Autistic spectrum kids really thrive from doing Brain Gym followed by song, dance and rhyming ... I spend whole sessions in that kind of play. Plus, games that encourage eye contact like peek-a-boo or light activation. Trampoline work with auditory directional cues like 'bounce right, bounce left.' Marbles and lawn-bowling type games where you have to hit a big target. Play-doh® and

Silly Putty® play before writing. Mazes and dot-to-dots on a big board. Guided visualizations to encourage imagery and comprehension."

– June Heinz, Director of the Abilities Family Learning Center/Educational Therapist

"The first thing I like to do with a new student is to gain their trust, and assure them that I love and accept them as they are. That doesn't mean there isn't room for change, but it does mean that we can both be open to the 'possibility' of change and, with that, improvement."

– Nadine Iba, Physical Therapist

"With clients I use Brain Gym on the occupational therapy equipment, like the 'scooter board,' skateboard, trampoline and physical therapy balls. Using stories for movements and processes like the Dennison Laterality Repatterning. Another activity I really enjoy is the fishing rod which is made using a short rod and attaching a piece of string to it with a magnet at the end. The client then has to pick up a 'fish' (a fish-shaped card with a picture that is often a Brain Gym activity) and then do the movement. We use this to practice finger movements, by using various methods to roll the string up or down, with fingers, wrist movement, one or two hands, etc."

– Marcelle Goldsmith Shaman, mother and Occupational Therapist/Brain Gym practitioner, co-author of Hands On: How to use Brain Gym® in the Classroom

"I find that all manner of fun and games that ask for deep pressure and heavy work is supportive to many children. I love *The Very Hungry Caterpillar* by Eric Carle. In this book, the caterpillar becomes a cocoon. In this part of the story, we all have a turn rolling up in a long piece of stretchy material to become a growing butterfly! The children push and wiggle and unroll out and then we have the material as our lovely butterfly wings! They experience lots of proprioception, tactile and vestibular stimulation in a non-threatening way. For those children that are not ready to lie down and roll into the fabric, I support them standing up and in other positions. For those

▲ **All ages like to play.**

that initially do not want to be wrapped, they usually change their minds and give it a go before the activity ends. These children really appreciate that snug feeling once they realize that the wrapping up is on their own terms (arms out and just a little wrapping, etc.).

The other day a group of 4- and 5 year-olds had a blast 'pushing and pulling' their little classmates in a large plastic storage tub. Several of these children have particular issues with hyper-active tactile systems, joining in with other children and eye contact. The 'heavy work' proprioception and vestibular movement of this kind of game really engaged ALL of the children as they waited for their turn, pushed or pulled the tub, and got to REALLY feel their bodies in the confines of the tub. Everyone was focused and playing as a team! I'm still grinning from ear to ear seeing their smiling faces looking at each other and me!"

– Libby Brandt, PT, Brain Gym® consultant

Balloon Crawling
Jon Bredal, MA, Educational Consultant

1. Children begin standing and hitting a balloon, then hitting a balloon with a partner.
2. Two children face each other sitting in cat-sit position and hit a balloon back and forth.
3. The children get on hands and knees and hit a balloon on the floor while it's on the floor and then up in the air.

4. The object is to keep hitting the balloon in the air until it is hit

into a basket or box placed on each end.

5. Players crawl with their heads up. They alternate hand to hit the balloon.

6. Players must have one hand on the floor at all times.

7. Two players hit a balloon back and forth to each other as they crawl toward one end.

8. Children get on their backs in a circle and kick the balloons around to each other.

9. Children slither like snakes on the floor while blowing a balloon. (Balloon Crawling really addresses the neck reflexes, ATNR and STNR, and is fun.)

"A favorite integrating activity that I use with students and clients is the Brain Gym® movement Double Doodle.[8-1] I was first introduced to this activity during a course with the co-founders of Brain Gym, Dr. Paul Dennison and his wife Gail. Double Doodle is a bilateral activity, which is done in the midfield to establish direction and orientation in space relative to the body. It activates the brain for hand-eye coordination, crossing the midline, visual discrimination and spatial awareness. It helps with academic skills of following directions, decoding and encoding written symbols as well as the subjects of writing, spelling, math and reading. The behavioral and postural correlations are left and right awareness,

▲ **Doing the Double Doodle.**

improved peripheral vision, body awareness, coordination and specialization of hands and eyes, and improved movement skills along with sports abilities.

In introducing the Double Doodle, the learner can be guided with their arms through a few simple movements. One can stand behind the person and move their arms while verbalizing, 'Out, in, up and down.' Once this is understood, a fun way to incorporate this with young learners is done in what I call, 'The

Mirror Game.' I tell the learners that we will play a game that is like we are looking into a mirror. The leader moves arms in various directions; up, down, out, in, circles one way then the other, then out and in crossing the midline. (If one hand is going out to the right, the other goes out to the left.) Perhaps the participant has seen the Looney Tunes® cartoon of Bugs Bunny as he tricks Elmer Fudd to believe he is seeing himself in the mirror, but it's really that rascally rabbit, Bugs.

Once learners have incorporated the feeling of the Double Doodle, they can do it tactilely on a carpet, or sand tray – graduating to holding writing implements in both hands and drawing on a whiteboard or paper taped to a table or wall while doing the movements. Besides drawing lines and circles, learners can do pictures and even write their names. Gail Dennison has created an entire class around this very movement."

– Natasha Gogin-Moses, Brain Gym® instructor and second grade teacher.

Client Story

"A lesson I have to keep learning all the time is that sometimes one tiny movement or success can make all the difference in the life of a child. It doesn't always take multiple methods, tests and sixty sessions!

A mother contacted me regarding her 2nd-grade son, whom I will call 'Danny.' Danny was having trouble writing, reading and performing in a timely manner in school. After screening him, it was obvious from his scores that he was well above second-grade skill level in every area. I couldn't find any visual or attention issues that would slow him down. So, I set an appointment to do a balance procedure. The teacher/parent in me always wants the student to pick the 'appropriate' goal. He's having trouble with schoolwork, so naturally he picks the goal of kicking the ball straight into the goal. I questioned him further to make sure we had paced this goal because I wasn't satisfied. Sure enough, he knew what he needed. It turns out the kids at school were making fun of him because he couldn't kick straight. He was on a soccer team and he'd get laughed at there, too. He was so nervous every day about recess and going to soccer practice that he couldn't sit still and focus on school.

Our pre-activity was kicking a ball down my very long, narrow hallway, at least 80 feet long. Danny couldn't decide which foot to kick with and, after some Optimal Brain Organization checks, I found he was pretty unbalanced. Boof, he'd kick the ball sideways and into a wall. He'd fall down before he could kick it. He'd kick it and it would roll, oh so slowly, maybe two feet. Meanwhile, he was frustrated, red and sweating. We went to work and ended up doing a Three Dimension Repatterning. After about 40 minutes, we went back out in the hall. Although I see this everyday, I was amazed and so was 'Danny.' His first kick went straight down the center of the hall, about halfway. He kicked with total confidence and was clearly right-foot dominant.

I set up a 3x3 box at the halfway point in our hallway and he hit the 'goal' the first time. I continued moving the box all the way to the hallway's end. He hit it every time. My screams of surprise only reinforced his own. We celebrated and his Mom joined in. He announced, 'Well, I'm all better, Mom. She fixed me.' I reminded him that he did it all by himself, but I'm not sure he bought it! Mom was really happy for Danny, but wondering how this would help in the classroom. I told her to let me know how things were going and we set up a time to meet. They took some homeplay moves with them: he selected the grounder and the calf-pump. She called each day with reports of success. Danny got an award that week from the teacher for several different areas of improvement. He made it on the chalkboard as Student of the Week. On Saturday, he made his first goal in a soccer game. It went on and on. When he arrived for his next appointment, he wanted to kick the ball down the hall for me. It went all the way down, 80 feet, dead center! Mom gave me a hug and we all did some Brain Gym together. I told them to call whenever they felt they needed me, but Danny reminded me that he was 'fixed.'

After a year I got a call. Danny was finishing up third grade with all A's and his soccer team was in the playoffs; he was the star player on the team. The only problem was that Danny had so many social engagements that Mom felt like a cab driver! Once again, I learned the lesson that kids know best when it comes to what they need."

– June Heinz, Director of the Abilities Family
Learning Center/Educational Therapist

Each of these activities from around the world provides another means for you to give the gift of yourself. Every quality moment spent with your child is a minute well spent building the foundation for their future. When your child needs you, be there for them. Our children come first! Your house doesn't always have to be spotless, with the laundry done and the dishes clean. Guess what? They will be messy and dirty again in no time.

If I Had My Child to Raise Over Again

If I had my child to raise all over again,

I'd finger paint more, and point the finger less.

I'd do less correcting, and more connecting.

I'd take my eyes off my watch, and watch with my eyes.

I would care to know less, and know to care more.

I'd take more hikes and fly more kites.

I'd stop playing serious, and seriously play.

I'd run through more fields and gaze at more stars.

I'd do more hugging, and less tugging.

I would be firm less often, and affirm much more.

I'd build self-esteem first, and the house later.

I'd teach less about the love of power,

And more about the power of love.

– By Diana Loomans © 8-2

A love of
learning!

**"For far too long teachers
have concentrated upon the
psychological problems of the child,
or the socio-economic environment,
instead of asking the question,
does the child have the equipment
which he needs to succeed at the
educational level asked of him and
methods imposed on him?"**

— A. E. Tansley

Ready for school with a love of learning !!!

Children will not be ready for school if they haven't completed
the necessary developmental patterns that lead them to the ability
to skip naturally with arms and legs swinging contralaterally.
If they have not experienced and integrated their horizontal,
vertical and three-dimensional concepts within their body and
sphere, they will have difficulty translating the up and down,
side to side, and circular motion required in the two-dimensional
media of books, paper, computers and the whiteboard of school.

When children can skip, they are ready to sit.

Some children go to school when they are not yet ready for the teacher's big rule "to sit still and not distract others with movement." The fact that they can't sit still is a reflection that their nervous system is not developed sufficiently for that difficult task. Could it be that they have not moved enough in the formative years with all of today's sedentary electronics? Their neurology is still developing and, ironically, movement is the key to that preparation for school. They are still learning to control the ability to balance. The most advanced form of balance is being still.

It is only when a child has control of movement that they can pay attention to other experiences. Unless children have satisfied that need within themselves to move, they will keep moving and "misbehaving." They are acting out their need and to them it feels like a craving. Just like with a sugar craving, unless the protein level in the body is balanced with the carbohydrate level, the person will keep craving sugar and eating more.

We must not deny today's children their nature. Denial of movement stunts their physical and emotional growth therefore their intellectual development. With all their natural movement, such as climbing on furniture and outside on anything that begs their innate curiosity like bleachers, rocks and trees, they are feeding themselves vestibular stimulation and learning postural muscle control, visual-motor integration and depth perception for visual development. If their behavior appears hyperactive, could they be sending us a loud message?

A child who is ready for kindergarten is ...

a child who can **physically**
- hop on one foot
- jump forward, taking off and landing with both feet
- skip, run and stop at will on a target
- have adequate hand-eye coordination
- bounce a ball with relative dexterity

a child who **recognizes**
- all primary colors
- shapes (circle, square, triangle, cross)
- letters of the alphabet

a child who **sees**
- similarities and differences in pictures and objects
- a circle, cross, square, or triangle and can copy it

a child who **listens**
- to directions without interrupting
- to stories and poems for five minutes without restlessness

a child who **hears**
- words that rhyme
- words that begin with the same sound, or different sounds
- a series of four numbers and can repeat them

a child who **speaks**
- and can look at books with pictures and pretend to read
- and can retell a short story or poem in correct sequence
- and can tell a story or relate an experience of their own

a child who **understands**
- the relationship inherent in such concepts as: up and down, in and out, over and under, fast and slow, top and bottom, hot and cold, empty and full, front and back.
- which is smaller? which is bigger? which one's different? which two are similar?
- the classification of words which represent people, places, and things

a child who **experiences**
- everyday activities and events commonplace for their peer group
- loving concern from adults around them

a child who **adjusts**
- to changes in routine and to new situations without becoming fearful
- to opposition or defeat without crying or sulking
- to the necessity of asking for help when needed

a child who **plays**
- cooperatively and respectfully with other children, taking turns
- and can share with others

a child who **shows interest**
- in numbers and counting objects
- in the letters of the alphabet

a child who **is able**
- to relax all body parts
- to follow directions
- to sit and stand quietly for a short period of time

a child who **has a good self-concept and loves life**

Getting Ready

Growth and development start from the head (cephalic) down and from the inside (core) out. If a child is unable to integrate the senses, they move inappropriately, feel uncomfortable in their body and have sensitivities. The vestibular system and the other senses, especially tactile, visual and auditory, must be properly functioning to have the ability to balance the body against gravity and succeed with academic skills like reading, writing and mathematics.

Impediments to a child's success are caused by interference in optimal communication between the brain and body. With proper learning tools, parents can facilitate the release of the physical, mental and emotional blocks and fill in the gaps of movement development that impair their child's best endeavor at peak performance. Once this happens, clear sensory messages will be able to travel from all parts of the body to the brain and back again in a loop. It is our job to provide the movement opportunities for children to move, grow and make more connections between the vestibular apparatus, core and the higher centers of the brain. With the little ones, enjoy rolling, crawling, swinging, rides in a wagon, or sling or on a bike that has a baby seat. For those children who can walk, add to that skipping, hopping, twirling, swinging, rolling down a hill, somersaults and cartwheels.

Whole learning

"When the core of the body is integrated, it provides the foundation for a stress-free, whole-learning experience." [9-2]

— Carol Ann Erickson

Primary Learning Tools

The Primary Learning Tools given throughout the book are ways that we can first awaken in our children the resources given by nature before addressing academic skills. If reflexes are not integrated, not matured, they will not be a support for future skills. A child who has trouble learning has a nervous system that is not processing information properly. Integrated reflexes, good motor development and physical skills are essential for noncompensatory success in school. All skills necessary in the classroom make use of the children's ability to use both their eyes and ears, knowledge of their body and its relationship to their surroundings. The awareness of such concepts as laterality, directionality and figure-ground must be developed in relation to the child's own body before they can be projected externally and used for the development of good reading, writing and math skills. Children learn from the inside out!

Good News

Fortunately, the importance of active movement is becoming more widespread. An article appeared in the *Bangor Daily News*, written by Mark Condon, titled "Cranial Calisthenics: Physical Exercise Stimulates Body and Mind."

> *It's Monday morning in Mrs. Rebecca Vigue's class at Washington Street Elementary in Brewer, Maine. Students just in from recess are preparing for the morning's lesson – writing in their journals about their Thanksgiving holiday. But instead of opening up their notebooks or sharpening their pencils, students in the class are doing something different, something you wouldn't expect in a classroom.*
>
> *They're moving. And no one is telling them to sit still.*
>
> *In front of a white chart of the alphabet written in cursive and near an American flag, two students lead the third-grade class through some introductory moves of Brain Gym®, a series of activities designed to help students get ready to learn. The students touch their left elbows to their right knees and right elbows to left knees ...*

More and more schools are using tools like Brain Gym® and hiring consultants like Beth Stoddard of Portland, Maine to present in-services so students (and teachers!) can benefit from whole-brain integration throughout the day. Children learn best with a curriculum that incorporate lots of movement to integrate the lesson plan of the day. When movement-based programs such as Brain Gym®/Educational Kinesiology, Education through Music®, Bal-a-vis-x® and S'Cool Moves for Learning™ are implemented into the school curriculum, lower-level movements and physical skills are addressed. These programs strive to foster well-balanced children with a well-organized and integrated brain.

Timing is Everything

Parents often struggle in their decision as to when to have their children start kindergarten. The cut-off date in California is December second, but the chronological date is not necessarily the best choice. If your child's birthday is in September, October or November and you have them start school at four years old, soon to be five, they may be one of the youngest students in the class. Why not give them one more year of movement play and development before entering the structure of school with its long hours? Particularly some children born in the summer need a little extra time to mature. This way, they will be six instead of five for kindergarten. Do not think that this means you are holding your child back or that they are anything less than smart! They will have a much stronger foundation and be better prepared for a positive experience.

What About Sports?

Playing sports is meant to be fun. You will be fortunate if your child has a coach that tells the players to "go out there and have some fun." After all, they are only little children. Sports can be very stressful for children if not properly monitored. We as parents want our children to succeed at whole-body activities like sports but not at their physical and emotional expense. The ball field is filled with intense, stressed-out parents yelling and criticizing their children from the sideline. Let us focus on relieving the pressure of competition.

If you like to make sports part of your child's experience, there are simple tools you can use to be supportive in a positive, encouraging way.

Sports

Before a game
• PACE/WBCH

During a game
• Xcel Thumbs-up
• The Hook-ups

After a game
• High-X-Ten

Before a Game

• **PACE/WBCH** – The Brain Gym PACE routine is a powerful way for you and your children to prepare for a game and get "in the zone." I call it "Tuning in to Radio Station WBCH" to make it easier to remember this order: **W**ater, **B**rain Buttons, **C**ross Crawl and **H**ook-ups. Start first by **Sipping Water** then rubbing **Brain Buttons** points (K 27s) in the soft spots just below the clavicle on both sides of the sternum while the other hand rests on the navel, followed by **Cross Crawl** (as described on page 81) and finish with **Hook-ups** (as described on page 41). This is a learning-readiness routine to

Tune In for Learning

WBCH is an acronym that stands for **W**ater, **B**rain Buttons, **C**ross Crawl and **H**ook-ups. This series of four movements, when done in this specific order, gets the brain/body system ready for learning or performing.

Water

Conducts the electrical transmissions throughout the body. Dehydration can trigger fuzzy short-term memory and difficulty focusing. 90% of our brain is water.

Brain Buttons

Supplies fresh oxygenated blood to the brain and increases lung/brain function. Relaxes tension of back neck muscles. Hand on navel draws attention to the center of the body activating vestibular/RAS/neocortex.

Cross Crawl

Activates and coordinates both hemispheres of the neocortex simultaneously. Done slowly, compels the frontal lobes into action and activates the vestibular system for balance.

Hook-Ups

Activates sensory and motor cortices in both hemispheres of the cerebrum simultaneously. The tongue connects the limbic system and the frontal lobes. The brain comes to an integrated state.

Remember to tune in to radio station WBCH to get connected for learning.

© Design by Denise Hornbeak; Graphic by Tammie Stimpfel; Compiled from Dr. Carla Hannaford's research; Based on Brain Gym® PACE sequence; Brain Gym® is a registered trademark of Brain Gym® International activate whole-brain function before any activity. After doing WBCH, you will all feel present in the moment, ready for the next activity with an integrated body and brain.

During a Game

- **Xcel Thumbs-up** – When you catch your player's eye, give them an Xcel Thumbs-up with both hands making fists and thumbs up while arms are crossed to form a big, integrated X. This can be your integrating symbol of encouragement!
- **The Hook-ups** – Described in detail on page 41 in Chapter 3. It is not unusual to see me doing Hook-ups on the bleachers or while standing on the sidelines at my son's games during a tense moment. We are all interconnected, so I know that calming myself will positively influence others.

▲ High-X-Ten.

After a Game

- **High-X-Ten** – A supportive recognition of your child's performance is to give them a High-X-Ten. Simply cross arms and clap each other's hands up high. This works great in many situations: athletic, academic, musical, theatrical, etc.

Does this really work?

During one soccer season, I introduced a few Brain Gym movements to my son's soccer team, the Riptides, at one of their practices using PACE and Thinking Caps. By the end of the season, the team was undefeated and was very excited to participate in the Ninth Annual Commissioner's Cup Youth Recreational Soccer Tournament Division 5. They won their first three games with the highest points of all 12 teams. It was amazing to watch their fancy footwork, strong kicks and how fast they could run up and down the field. Winning those three games put them into the Semi-Finals against a really rough and tough behaving team. Kevin scored the first goal of the Semi-Final game from the midfield with his "Surprise" left foot. When he whacked the ball, it went sailing halfway across the field and landed in the goal.

By the end of the game it was tied 2-2, which meant they had to shoot Penalty Picks (PKs). (Five members from each team are picked by the coach to shoot the ball into the goal being defended by the opponent's goalie.) At this point, practically all the Riptide boys were in tears because the game had become inordinately rough due to being loosely called by the referees, creating a very high-stress, unsafe athletic atmosphere. Our boys were also remembering the sad ending to the previous season when they had lost a qualifier in the pouring rain by Penalty Kicks. All-in-all, a recipe for panic, negativity, and overwhelm! Believe me, I was doing Hook-Ups along with some of the other parents during the Penalty Kicks. I was so proud of Kevin (just turned age 9) because he volunteered to kick first and aced it in the goal! Then the other team's kicker missed his goal with our dynamite goalie defending our position. Our next two players shot goals to win that game and take us to the Championship game, which was to start in 40 minutes. The kids and parents asked me to do Brain Gym with our Stars before the last game. I was so pleased the request came forth from them! The Riptides won the Commissioner's Cup Championship game 3-0.

We've been singing and playing the song "We are the Champions" a lot ever since. Actually, I had the whole team humming it during Hook-ups before that last championship game! No question, I'm the Proud Mom of an Integrated, Athletic, Brain Gym model of a son.

From Delivery Room to Classroom

As I reflect on my passion to share valuable Primary Learning Tools for children's success and happiness, I wish to convey that it CAN be an exciting journey every step of the way. Even with the challenges — and there will be plenty throughout the years — all can be worked out, making you a stronger and more patient parent, and bring you closer and more connected to your loved ones.

Each stage is precious in its moment and I always celebrated the wonder of each year. Some people say, "Just wait until they are older; it will get easier and be better." You don't have to wait for the future. I have no favorite age. They have all been *fantabulous*! Every age is magical in its own special way!

In the early years I naturally did activities recommended for children with special needs because they address sensory integration and vestibular stimulation, which are of vital importance for any child. Why not play the games and movement activities (Primary Learning Tools) routinely and automatically to enhance brain development so the gaps are filled in before most challenges arise and thereby avoiding a lifetime of being labeled.

Children have so much potential innocently waiting to be drawn out so they can function more easily and be prepared for kindergarten. By starting the PLTs early in their young lives, there are possibilities for great accomplishments. And even if you were unaware of these tools and your child is now 6-years-old or older and struggling in school, take the time to experience a few suggestions each month. Find the ones that will become your child's pals — those activities that make them feel calmer and more centered in their body — those movements that wake up the brain-body connection for ease in learning.

The Primary Learning Tools can enhance
- memory
- listening skills
- singing
- artistic and musical ability
- cooperative behavior
- self-confidence
- physical coordination
- the desire to learn
- focusing ability
- academic skills

Bringing it Home

As a parent, it's easy to become overwhelmed by all the things you could possibly do. My hope is that you'll choose a few things from this book that resonate with you, and then a few more. My greatest testimony for the methods I have presented to you is my son. By age seven, Kevin had experienced a myriad of movements including a few Brain Gym activities, especially

"Radio Station WBCH." Kevin is a phenomenal reader, writer, speller, mathematician, artist and athlete. He truly was and continues to be a model of a SuperConfitelligent Child.

I was complimenting Kevin on how grateful I am that he is responsible for getting his homework done. Recently he told his Dad that he didn't want to stay very long at the restaurant because he had a lot of homework due the next day. After I complimented him and mentioned that this would be something important to put in the final chapter of this book, Kevin had a message for children. He said, "Your family won't feel very stressed-out if you are very responsible for things like homework." Because he is truly an integrated child, he doesn't feel overwhelmed with homework and enjoys doing it. But of course, recess is his favorite time in school.

> ## Move for Success
>
> "What children experience at home in the early years of life becomes the irreplaceable foundation and springboard for success in school, the arts, sports and ultimately all aspects of life!"

Let your child feel their responsibility. Each child has an intuitive knowingness in their body/mind system whispering what is best for them. Teach them to notice, listen, acknowledge and choose the "right" action. Or choose again. Another example is Anastasia's parents (from chapter four) who have held the space so that her instinctive sense could be drawn out. In making a choice, Anastasia says, "My heart tells me this." How precious!

Final Thoughts

During the years before kindergarten, parents and caregivers will have unlimited opportunities to contribute to the enrichment of young children's growth and development. This preparation begins early and has an everlasting impact on all levels including the emotional, intellectual and physical levels for the rest of their lives. It can be a time that serves their growth as an individual, not only academically but also as a whole person — giving them a loving, strong and safe foundation to move forward into school — knowing that learning is one of life's most exciting and fulfilling activities.

> ## Learning
>
> "Learning is one of Life's most exciting and fulfilling activities."

Parents CAN make a significant difference in their child's life. We have the opportunity to facilitate children generating new neural networks in the midst of play. We can also create an environment conducive to learning and to doing their very best.

It will take courage, creativity and patience.
- Patience for us to let our children explore with their senses
- Patience to let them make mistakes
- Patience to allow them to express their true essence

The Primary Learning Tools described throughout this book are the foundation for future success. It truly is up to us! It's the power behind the performance: as children transition into school empowered with the skills learned through movement and play, they have the potential to sit comfortably in any classroom while fully hearing, seeing and processing new information as well as enthusiastically communicating the knowledge they are learning.

What is the result? A Super - Confident - Intelligent and Happy Child who feels secure from the inside out and who is truly ready for the new adventure of school as well as for the journey of a lifelong love of learning!

The *SuperConfitelligent* child flourishes when moving and playing. These active experiences in the early years of life become the irreplaceable foundation and springboard for success in school and all aspects of life!

PLTs

Below are the page references to all Primary Learning Tools (PLTs) in the book. PLTs are the cornerstone to raising and educating a SuperConfitelligent Child.

- Activities for Auditory Processing..99
- Activities for the Olfactory System 92
- Activities for the Proprioceptive Sense................................94
- Activities for Receptive Touch...86
- Activities to instill a Steady Beat..102
- Activities for Taste Perception 91
- Activities to integrate the skills of Visual Development 113
- Activities for Visual-Perceptual Processing.......................110
- Creative Play Activities 73
- Developmental Movement Patterns....................................67
- Infant PLTs 55
- Pausing Moment Activities
    to raise Self-Esteem 126
    for those Upset Times...121
- Playful Games...4
- PLTs for Life 56
- PLTs promoting Motor Development 70
- Reality-Based Play Toys..74
- Top Ten Tension Tamers..37
- Vestibular Activities 83
- WBCH (Tune in for Learning Chart)....................................155
- Writing-Prep Activities 7
- 33 Ways to Encourage a Child 125

Endnotes

Introduction

i   "School Readiness Backgrounder" (March 2003) Available from Getting School Ready, http://www.gettingschoolready.org/gsrbackground.html.

ii   Zaslow, M. Calkins, J. and Halle, T. "Child Trends-Background for Community Level Work on School Readiness: a Review of Definitions, Assessments and Investment Strategies." (Report for Knights Foundation) 2000.

Chapter 1: Your Role As Teacher

1-1   Dr Paul Dennison, founder of Brain Gym® International, named this activity, Energy Yawn. www.braingym.org.

1-2   Ronin-Walknowska, Elzbieta and Masgutova, Svetlana. *Movement Secrets of the Utero Life*. DVD and "Birthing Reflexes" course notes, August 2006.

1-3   Cohen, Isabel and Marcelle Goldsmith. *Hands On: How to use Brain Gym® in the Classroom*. Ventura, CA: Edu-Kinesthetics, 2000. p. 21. Available at www.denisehornbeak.com.

1-4   Evolving Art is adapted from the activity, Contour Drawing, which I first learned at an Educational Kinesiology course called "Visioncircles."

1-5   Masgutova, Svetlana. "Integration of Dynamic and Postural Reflexes" course notes, August 2004.

1-6   Cohen, Isabel and Marcelle Goldsmith. *Hands On: How to use Brain Gym® in the Classroom*. For more details contact Purpose Play at hands-on@mweb.co.za.

Chapter 2: Brain Plasticity

2-1   Brain Gym® is a registered trademark of the Educational Kinesiology Foundation. Brain Gym® International, 1575 Spinnaker Dr., Ste.204B, Ventura, CA 93001. (800) 356-2109 www.braingym.org.

2-2   Eliot, Lise. *What's Going On in There?* New York, NY: Bantam Books, 1999. pp. 424-425.

2-3   Ibid. pp. 6, 8, 35.

2-4   Spitz, Renë. *Dialogues from Infancy: Selected Papers*. edited by R.N. Emde. New York, NY: International Universities Press, 1983.

2-5   Kempermann, Gerd and Fred Gage. "New Nerve Cells for the Adult Brain." *Scientific American,* May, 1999.

2-6   Kempermann, Gerd, George,Kuhn and Fred Gage. "More Hippocampal Neurons in Adult Mice Living in an Enriched

Environment." *Nature, Vol.* 386, April 3, 1997. pp. 493-495.

2-7   Van Praag, Henriette et al. ***Running Increases Cell Proliferation and Neurogenesis in the Adult Mouse Dentate Gyrus.*** *Nature Neuroscience, Vol.* 2, No. 3, March 1999. pp. 266-270.

2-8   Hannaford, Carla. ***Smart Moves, Why Learning Is Not All in Your Head.*** Salt Lake City, UT: Great River Books, 2005. p. 132.

2-9   Eliot, Lise. ***What's Going On In There?*** New York, NY: Bantam Books, 1999. p. 4.

2-10   Hannaford, Carla. ***Smart Moves, Why Learning Is Not All in Your Head.*** Salt Lake City, UT: Great River Books, 2005. pp. 23, 28.

2-11   Experts in the field: Nancy Tappe, Lee Carroll, Jan Tober and Doreen Virtue.

2-12   Carroll, L., and Tober, J. ***The Indigo Children-The New Kids Have Arrived.*** Santa Monica, CA: Hay House, 1999. p.1.

2-13   Tappe, Nancy. Lecture notes 9/27/02 and 10/19/02.

2-14   Virtue, Doreen. ***The Crystal Children.*** Santa Monica, CA: Hay House, 2003. p. 3-4.

2-15   Ibid. pp. 7-8.

Chapter 3: Brain Inhibitors To Learning

3-1   Hannaford, Carla. ***Awakening the Child Heart, Handbook for Global Parenting.*** Hawaii: Jamilla Nur Pub., 2002. p. 57.

3-2   Hannaford, Carla. Personal Communication. Apr. 2, 2007.

3-3   Book comp body15i.qx 6/15/06, p. 12.

3-4   Healy, Jane. ***Failure to connect: how computers affect our children's minds--for better and worse.*** New York, NY: Simon and Schuster. 1998.

3-5   Hannaford, Carla. ***Smart Moves, Why Learning Is Not All in Your Head.*** Salt Lake City, UT: Great River Books, 2005. p. 18.

3-6   Christakis, D. A., et. al., "Early Television Exposure and Subsequent Attentional Problems in Children." *Pediatrics*, April 2004 (*Vol.* 113 No. 4), pp. 708-713.

3-7   American Academy of Pediatrics. *Television: How it Affects Children.* http://www.aap.org/healthtopics/mediause.cfm, 2002.

3-8   Nielsen Media Research http://www.cdtv.net/users/node/8754.

3-9   Jordan, A., et, al. "Reducing Children's Television-Viewing Time." *Pediatrics*, November 2006 (*Vol.* 118 No. 5), pp. e1303-e1310 (doi:10.1542/peds.2006-0732.)

3-10   Hannaford, Carla. ***Smart Moves, Why Learning Is Not All in Your Head.*** Salt Lake City, UT: Great River Books, 2005. pp. 52, 76.

3-11   American Academy of Pediatrics. "Television: How it Affects Children." http://www.aap.org/healthtopics/mediause.cfm, 2002.

3-12   Committee on Public Education. "Children, adolescents, and television." *Journal of the American Academy of Pediatrics*, 107(2), February 2001. pp. 423-426.

3-13   Batmanghelidji, F. *Your Body's Many Cries for Water*. Falls Church, VA: Global Health Solutions, 1993.

3-14   Hannaford, Carla. *Smart Moves, Why Learning Is Not All in Your Head*. Salt Lake City, UT: Great River Books, 2005. p. 156.

3-15   Colombo, Marcio F.; Donald C. Rau and V. Adrian Parsegian. "Protein Solvation in Allosteric Regulation: A Water Effect on Hemoglobin." *Science*, May 1, 1992 (*vol*. 256), pp. 655-659.

3-16   Hannaford, Carla. *Smart Moves, Why Learning Is Not All in Your Head*. Salt Lake City, UT: Great River Books, 2005. p. 151.

3-17   Stratton, Bill. Personal Communication. "The Feel-Good-Again Polarity Practice." 1823 Forestdale Dr., Encinitas CA 92024. Phone: 760-479-1678. Website: www.billstratton.com. Email: billstratton911@aol.com. Energy Balancing - Intuitive Healing.

3-18   Hobson, Caroline. Personal Communication. Weaverville, NC. chobson11@yahoo.com.

3-19   Stratton, Bill. Personal Communication. "The Feel-Good-Again Polarity Practice." 1823 Forestdale Dr., Encinitas CA 92024. Phone: 760-479-1678. Website: www.billstratton.com. Email: billstratton911@aol.com. Energy Balancing - Intuitive Healing.

3-20   Dennison, Paul. *Brain Gym® and Me*. Ventura, CA: Edu-Kinesthetics, Inc., 2006. p. 46.

3-21   Ayres, A. Jean. *Sensory Integration and the Child*. Los Angeles, CA: Western Psychological Services, 1989. pp. 14-15.

3-22   Hannaford, Carla. *Smart Moves, Why Learning Is Not All in Your Head*. Salt Lake City, UT: Great River Books, 2005. p. 111.

3-23   Randolph, Shirley, and Heiniger, Margot. *Kids Learn From The Inside Out*. Boise, ID: Legendary Publishing CO., 1998. pp. 13-14.

3-24   Brody, J. E. "Baby Walkers May Slow Infants' Development." *New York Times*, October 14, 1997. p. 18.

3-25   Hannaford, Carla. *Smart Moves, Why Learning Is Not All in Your Head*. Salt Lake City, UT: Great River Books, 2005. p. 112.

Chapter 4: Reflexes As Foundational

4-1   Hocking, Claire. *Childhood Reflexes and their Effect on Learning and Behavior*. Wendouree, Victoria/Australia, 2002. p. 3.

4-2   Notes from Dr. Svetlana Masgutova's course, "Integration of Dynamic and Postural Reflexes into the Whole Body Movement System." 2004. www.masgutovamethod.com.

4-3   Randolph, Shirley, and Heiniger, Margot. *Kids Learn From The Inside Out*. Boise, ID: Legendary Publishing CO., 1998. p. 6.

4-4   Hoppe, Diana, M.D. Electronic communication. March 1, 2007.

4-5   Masgutova, Svetlana. *Integration of Dynamic and Postural Reflexes into the Whole Body Movement System*. Poland:

International NeuroKinesiology Institute of Movement Development and Reflex Integration™, 2004. p. 71.

4-6   Ibid. p. 37.

4-7   Hocking, Claire. *Childhood Reflexes and their Effect on Learning and Behavior*. Wendouree, Victoria/Australia, 2002. pp, 24-25, 58-59, 70-71.

4-8   Notes from Dr. Svetlana Masgutova's course, "Integration of Dynamic and Postural Reflexes into the Whole Body Movement System." 2004.

4-9   Masgutova, Svetlana. *Integration of Dynamic and Postural Reflexes into the Whole Body Movement System*. Poland: International NeuroKinesiology Institute of Movement Development and Reflex Integration™, 2004. p. 66.

4-10   This is a modification of the Brain Gym activity, called the Calf Pump. www.braingym.org.

4-11   Hobson, Caroline. Personal Communication. Weaverville, NC. chobson11@yahoo.com. October 14, 2006.

4-12   www.masgutovamethod.com and www.braingym.org.

4-13   as cited in Heiberger, Debra, and Heiniger-White, Margot. *S'cool Moves for Learning*. Shasta, CA: Integrated Learner Press, 2000. p. 169.

4-14   Foster, W. J. *I Can Run, I Can Read*. Houston, TX: Education Media, Ltd., 1988. pp. 4-5.

4-15   Masgutova, Svetlana. *Integration of Dynamic and Postural Reflexes into the Whole Body Movement System*. Poland: International NeuroKinesiology Institute of Movement Development and Reflex Integration™, 2004. pp. 45, 60-61.

4-16   Ibid. p. 66.

4-17   Notes from Carol Ann Erickson's course, "Brain Gym for Educators," 2001.

4-18   Blomberg, Harald, M.D. *Rhythmic Movement Training* course manual. 2007, pp. 10, 14. www.haraldblomberg.com.

4-19   Cohen, Barbara Bainbridge. *Sensing, Feeling, and Action*. Northampton, MA: Contact Editions, 1993. p. 108.

4-20   Crazy Straw is only one of many activities that The HANDLE® Institute International uses in their approach. www.handle.org. (206) 204-6000.

4-21   Garbourg, Paula. *The Secret of the Ring Muscles: Healing Yourself through Sphincter Exercise*. Garden City Park, NY: Avery Publ. Group, 1997.

Chapter 5: Movement Is The Link To Learning

5-1   Ayres, A. Jean. *Sensory Integration and the Child*. Los Angeles, CA: Western Psychological Services, 1989. p. 141.

5-2 White, Ann. "Why Good Motor Development Is Important." http:/www.center4success.com, 1999.

5-3 Ibid.

5-4 Dennison, Paul. *Brain Gym® and Me*. Ventura, CA: Edu-Kinesthetics, Inc., 2006. pp. 90-91.

5-5 Cohen, Barbara Bainbridge. *Sensing, Feeling, and Action.* Northampton, MA: Contact Editions, 1993. p. 5.

5-6 Erickson, Carol Ann. *Movement Exploration* course manual. West Palm Beach, Florida: lifehanc@aol.com 973-600-0372, 1997. pp.14-38.

5-7 Erickson, Carol Ann. *Movement Exploration* course manual 1997. pp. 1-18. *Good Night Limbs* and *Mouse Hunting for Cheese* are my story-form variations of the basic navel radiation activity by Carol Ann Erickson.

5-8 Cohen, Barbara Bainbridge. *Sensing, Feeling, and Action.* Northampton, MA: Contact Editions, 1993. p. 105.

5-9 Carter, Rita. *Mapping the Mind*, Berkeley, CA: The University of California Press, 2000.

5-10 Dennison, Gail. personal communication, April 29, 2002.

5-11 Hannaford, Carla. *Awakening the Child Heart, Handbook for Global Parenting*. Hawaii: Jamilla Nur Pub., 2002. p. 120.

5-12 as cited in Dancy, Rahima Baldwin. *You are your Child's First Teacher*. Berkeley, CA: Celestial Arts, 2000. p. 186.

5-13 Dancy, Rahima Baldwin. *You are your Child's First Teacher*. Berkeley, CA: Celestial Arts, 2000. p. 165.

5-14 as cited in Tangley, L. "Animal emotions." *US News and World Report*. March 8, 2001. p. 383.

5-15 Hannaford, Carla. *Awakening the Child Heart, Handbook for Global Parenting*. Hawaii: Jamilla Nur Pub., 2002. p. 122.

5-16 Ayres, A. Jean. *Sensory Integration and the Child*. Los Angeles, CA: Western Psychological Services, 1989. p. 167.

5-17 Ibid. p. 169. and Hannaford, Carla. *Smart Moves*... 2005. p. 46.

5-18 Hannaford, Carla. *Awakening the Child Heart, Handbook for Global Parenting*. Hawaii: Jamilla Nur Pub., 2002. p. 125. Hannaford, Carla. *Smart Moves, Why Learning Is Not All in Your Head*. 2005. p. 46.

5-19 Pearce, J. C. *Evolutions End: Claiming The Potential Of Our Intelligence*. San Francisco, CA: Harper, 1993. p. 162.

5-20 Dancy, Rahima Baldwin. *You are your Child's First Teacher*. Berkeley, CA: Celestial Arts, 2000. p.174.

Chapter 6: Making Sense Of The Senses

6-1 Purves D, Augustine G, Fitzpatrick D, et al. *Neuroscience* Second Edition. Massachusetts: Sinauer Associates, Inc, 2001.

6-2   Eliot, Lise. *What's Going on in There?* New York, NY: Bantam Books, 1999. p. 149.

6-3   Goddard, Sally. *Reflexes, Learning and Behavior*. Eugene, OR: Fern Ridge Press, 2002. pp. 56, 57, 159.

6-4   Hannaford, Carla. *Smart Moves, Why Learning Is Not All in Your Head*. Salt Lake City, UT: Great River Books, 2005. p. 38.

6-5   Eliot, Lise. *What's Going on in There?* New York, NY: Bantam Books, 1999. p. 147.

6-6   Ibid. p. 156.

6-7   Ibid. p. 154.

6-8   Clark, D. L. et al. "Vestibular Stimulation Influence On Motor Development In Infants." *Science,* 1977 (*vol.* 196), pp. 1228-1229.

6-9   Goddard, Sally. *Reflexes, Learning and Behavior*. Eugene, Oregon: Fern Ridge Press, 2002. p. 159.

6-10   Ibid. p. 160.

6-11   Hannaford, Carla. *Smart Moves, Why Learning Is Not All in Your Head*. Salt Lake City, UT: Great River Books, 2005. pp. 172-173.

6-12   Dennison, Paul and Gail Dennison, *Brain Gym, Teachers Edition*. Ventura, CA: Edu-Kinesthetics, Inc., 1994. p. 8.

6-13   http://en.wikipedia.org/wiki/Reticular_activating_system.

6-14   Eliot, Lise. *What's Going on in There?* New York, NY: Bantam Books, 1999. p. 123.

6-15   Hannaford, Carla. *Awakening the Child Heart, Handbook for Global Parenting*. Hawaii: Jamilla Nur Pub., 2002. p. 58.

6-16   Prescott, James. "Jailing Mothers Is Always Too-Harsh Justice." *The New York Times*. August 21, 1996.

6-17   Prescott, James. *Bulletin of the Atomic Scientists*, November, 1975. p. 11.

6-18   Harlow, H.F., and Zimmerman, R.R. "Affectional Responses in the Infant Monkey." *Science*, 1959 (*vol.* 130), pp. 421-32.

6-19   Masgutova, S. "My Inner Child: Integration of Lifelong Reflexes into Movement Development" course, August 2005.

6-20   Wennekes, Renate. Institut für Kinesiologische Lernförderung, Hinnenkamper Strabe 11,49434 Neuenkirchen-Vörden, Germany.

6-21   Eliot, Lise. *What's Going on in There?* New York, NY: Bantam Books, 1999. p. 127.

6-22   Ibid. pp. 123, 144.

6-23   Compiled by Tim Jacob, Cardiff University, U.K. http://www.cf.ac.uk/biosi/staff/jacob/teaching/sensory/taste.html.

6-24   Eliot, Lise. *What's Going on in There?* New York, NY: Bantam Books, 1999. p. 174. and http://www.cf.ac.uk/biosi/staff/jacob/teaching/sensory/taste.html.

6-25   Cohen, Barbara Bainbridge. *Sensing, Feeling, and Action.*

Northampton, MA: Contact Editions, 1993.

6-26　Buck, Linda and Richard Axel. (1991). "A Novel Multigene Family May Encode Odorant Receptors: A Molecular Basis for Odor Recognition." *Cell* 65:175-183. http://en.wikipedia.org/wiki/Olfaction.

6-27　Edwards, Rita. *In-Synch 1: Integrating the Senses through Movement*. Spectrum Whole Person Training, 2004. p. 65.

6-28　Upledger, John. *A Brain is Born*. Berkeley, CA: North Atlantic Books, 1996. p. 115.

6-29　Eliot, Lise. *What's Going on in There?* New York, NY: Bantam Books, 1999. pp. 229-230.

6-30　Damasio, Antonio R. *Descartes' Error: Emotion, Reason, and the Human Brain*. NY: Putnam, 1994. pp. 112-113.

6-31　Eliot, Lise. *What's Going on in There?* New York, NY: Bantam Books, 1999. pp. 240-241.

6-32　Hannaford, Carla. *Smart Moves, Why Learning Is Not All in Your Head*. Salt Lake City, UT: Great River Books, 2005. p. 43.

6-33　Eliot, Lise. *What's Going on in There?* New York, NY: Bantam Books, 1999. pp. 251-252.

6-34　Ibid. pp. 257-258.

6-35　Gracey, K. "Current Concepts In Universal Newborn Hearing Screening And Early Hearing Detection And Intervention Programs." *Advances in Neonatal Care*, 2003. 3(6), pp. 308-317.

6-36　Goddard, Sally. *Reflexes, Learning and Behavior*. Eugene, Oregon: Fern Ridge Press, 2002. p. 69.

6-37　Storr, A. *Music and the Mind*. London: Harper Collins, 1993. pp. 77-85.

6-38　Goddard, Sally. *Reflexes, Learning and Behavior*. Eugene, Oregon: Fern Ridge Press, 2002. p. 65.

6-39　Bowlus, Jean. Licensed Speech Language Pathologist. personal communication. April 28, 2007.

6-40　Goddard, Sally. *Reflexes, Learning and Behavior*. Eugene, Oregon: Fern Ridge Press, 2002. p. 67.

6-41　Masgutova, Svetlana. *Facial Reflexes Integration: NeuroKinesiology for Children and Adults to Encourage Their Speech and Motor Development*. Presented at the "Facial Reflexes" course, Carlsbad, CA. August, 2006.

6-42　Ibid.

6-42　Hannaford, Carla. "Physiological Basis of Learning" course, June 2000.

6-43　Heiberger, Debra, and Heiniger-White, Margot. *S'cool Moves for Learning*. Shasta, CA: Integrated Learner Press, 2000. pp. 111-112.

6-44 Dennison, Paul and Gail Dennison, **Brain Gym, Teachers Edition**. Ventura, CA: Edu-Kinesthetics, Inc., 1994. p.8.

6-45 Ibid. p. 30.

6-46 Hannaford, Carla. **Awakening the Child Heart, Handbook for Global Parenting**. Hawaii: Jamilla Nur Pub., 2002. p. 99.

6-47 Ibid. p. 97.

6-48 Thompson, Melody and Ownbey, Marian. "Music and Movement: Orchestrating Brain Gym in Any Classroom" workshop. Routine 1: Music, Music, Music Simplified Rhythm Stick Activities, "Celebration" **Kid's dance Party, Vol. 3** Routine 2: "Heartbeat," Lee Campbell-Towell/Cat Paws in Motion, **Any Turkey Can Tango**, www.mycatpaws.com; "Fun, Fun, Fun" and "I Get Around," The Beach Boys.

6-49 www.educationthroughmovement.com.

6-50 Goddard, Sally. **Reflexes, Learning and Behavior**. Eugene, Oregon: Fern Ridge Press, 2002. p. 69.

6-51 Ibid. p. 70.

6-52 Hannaford, Carla. **Smart Moves, Why Learning Is Not All in Your Head**. Salt Lake City, UT: Great River Books, 2005. p. 119.

6-53 Healy, Jane, **Failure to connect: how computers affect our children's minds--for better and worse**. New York, NY: Simon and Schuster, 1998. pp. 117, 228.

6-54 Blakemore, C., and Cooper, G. F. "Development of the Brain Depends on the Visual Environment." **Nature**, 1970 (*vol.* 228), pp. 477-78.

6-55 Wiesel, T. N. "Postnatal Development of the Visual Cortex and the Influence of Environment." **Nature**, 1982. (*vol.* 299), pp. 583-91.

6-56 Eliot, Lise. **What's Going on in There?** New York, NY: Bantam Books, 1999. pp. 196, 203, 208-210.

6-57 Goddard, Sally. **Reflexes, Learning and Behavior**. Eugene, Oregon: Fern Ridge Press, 2002. pp. 70-72.

6-58 Anshel, Jeffrey, **Smart Medicine for Your Eyes**. New York, NY: Avery. 1999. pp. 13, 18.

6-59 "Ophthalmologists Are Alarmed by the Number of Children Who Do Not Receive Vision Screenings; Screenings Detect the Number One Blinding Eye Disorder." http://home.businesswire.com/portal/site/google/index.jsp?ndmViewId=news_view&newsId=20070328005331&newsLang=en

6-60 Anshel, Jeffrey, **Smart Medicine for Your Eyes.** New York, NY: Avery, 1999. p. 17.

6-61 Bal-A-Vis-X. Information http://www.bal-a-vis-x.com.

6-62 Eliot, Lise. **What's Going on in There?** New York, NY: Bantam Books, 1999. p. 227.

6-63   Kodiak, Eve. *Rappin' on the Reflexes: A Practical Guide to Infant Reflexes*. Sound Intelligence Productions, P.O. Box 13, Temple, NH, 03084, 2005. pp. 57-59. www.evekodiak.com.

6-64   Ayres, A. Jean. *Sensory Integration and the Child*. Los Angeles, CA: Western Psychological Services, 1989. p. 167.

6-65   Ibid. p. 7.

Chapter 7: Guiding Your Child's Spirit

7-1   Thie, John and Matthew Thie, *Touch for Health: A Practical Guide to Natural Health with Acupressure, Touch and Massage*. Camarillo, CA: DeVorss Publication, 2005. p. 52.

7-2   Hannaford, Carla. Personal communication, May 4, 2007.

7-3   Wynne, Laura. Interview. Sedona, AZ, July 3, 2006. (928) 204-1704.

7-4   Roixen, Michael and Mehmet Oz, *You on a Diet*. New York, NY: Free Press, 2006. Oz, Mehmet The *Oprah Winfrey* show, November 29, 2006.

7-5   Wynne, Laura. Interview. Sedona, AZ, July 3, 2006. (928) 204-1704.

7-6   Ibid.

7-7   Dennison, Paul and Gail Dennison, *Brain Gym, Teachers Edition*. Ventura, CA: Edu-Kinesthetics, Inc., 1994. p. 6.

7-8   Thompson, C. and Rudolph, L. *Counseling Children* (3rd ed.) Pacific Grove, CA: Brooks-Cole, 1992. p. 192.

Chapter 8: Favorite Connecting Activities

8-1   Some information used in this excerpt is from *Brain Gym*® *Teacher's Edition* by Paul E. Dennison Ph.D. and Gail Dennison© 1994.

8-2   Loomans, Diana. *100 ways to Build Self-Esteem and Teach Values*. Tiburon, CA: New World Library. 1994. p. 216. www. dianaloomans.com.

Chapter 9: A Love Of Learning

9-1   As cited in Goddard, Sally. *Reflexes, Learning and Behavior*. Eugene, Oregon: Fern Ridge Press, 2002. p. 131.

9-2   Erickson, Carol Ann. *Movement Exploration* course manual. West Palm Beach, Florida, 1997. p. 1-1. lifehanc@aol.com 973-600-0372.

Index

A

ADD, 27, 56, 64, 83
ADHD, 27, 56, 64, 72, 83, 100
Adrenaline, 19, 30, 47
Alcohol, 38, 43, 96, 122
Aloha-ha-ha, 37, 40
Alzheimer's Disease, 83
Aminoglycosides, 79
Amygdala, 91
Antibiotics, 43, 79, 96
Apoptosis, 69, 108
Articulation, 50, 55, 59
Asphyxia, 96
Ataxia, 62
ATNR, 47, 48, 52, 66, 145
Attention, 7, 20, 23, 27, 33, 58, 64, 67,
    76, 80-83, 86, 97, 102, 113, 127,
    128, 137, 146, 150, 155
Audition, 95
Auditory, 24, 29, 34, 43, 46, 51, 58, 71,
    78, 81, 82, 95-98, 100-102, 104,
    113, 116, 118, 142, 152
    discrimination, 98, 100, 104
    processing, 100, 104, 163
Autism, 5, 27, 32, 47, 64, 80, 86, 100,
    142
Autistic behaviors/symptoms, 4, 38,
    85, 86

B

Babinsky reflex, 47, 48
Back roller, 37, 40, 94
Bal-A-Vis-X, 111, 153
Balance, viii, 7, 37, 39, 41, 42, 46,
    52-55, 58, 59, 62, 69, 78-82, 112,
    130, 131, 139, 140, 150, 152, 153,
    155
Balance board, 111
Balloon Crawling, 144, 145
Beanbag, 72, 73, 111

Binocular, 43, 58, 108, 113
Birth, 20, 22, 24, 47-50, 56, 65, 69, 70,
    78, 84, 85, 91, 96, 97, 107, 108,
    128
Bladder, 53, 54, 59
Body awareness, 41, 54, 83, 93, 145
Bonding, 15, 20, 24, 48, 49, 85, 134
Bouncer, vii, 50
Bowel & bladder control, 54, 59
Brain
    development, 22, 28, 33, 42, 46,
    70, 79, 158
    growth, 22, 84
    plasticity, 20, 22, 28
Brain Gym®, 4, 5, 14, 17, 18, 35-37,
    47, 55, 71, 81, 112, 119, 127, 128,
    134, 136, 138-140, 142, 143, 145,
    147, 153-158
Breast-feed, 49, 113
Breathing, 2, 3, 24, 29, 37-40, 50, 59,
    65, 66, 68, 102, 117, 122
Broca's area, 55
Burrito, 86-88

C

C-Section/Cesarean, 49, 50, 56
Car Wash, 86, 88, 89
Caressing, 85, 86
Carrying infants, 86, 87
Cerebellum, 20, 23, 57, 62, 79, 88
Cerebral cortex, 93, 95, 108
Cerebrum, 29, 155
Circle games, 70
Clapping-Tapping game, 101
Cochlea, 78, 95
Colors, 3, 5, 113, 114, 135, 137
Competition, vi, 32, 154
Computers, 33, 34, 105, 106, 149
Conception, vii, 19, 30, 46, 47, 79, 95,
    102, 107, 128
Contralateral, 66-69, 118, 149

Cortisol, 19, 30, 47
Crab, 7, 8
Crawling, 4, 24, 43, 48, 51, 57, 62, 63, 67, 70, 71, 74, 75, 80, 82, 94, 134, 141, 144, 145, 152
Crazy straw, 57-59
Cross Crawl, 71, 81-83, 113, 139, 154, 155
Cross-lateral activity, 43, 54, 75, 81, 118
Crossed-eyes, 59
Crystal children, 24-27

D

Dance, 102, 104, 134, 135, 139, 142
Deafness, 79
Deep pressure, 41, 87, 94, 143
Dehydration, 38, 155
Dennison Laterality Repatterning, 64, 143
Destressors, 37
Development, vi-viii, 7, 15, 22, 24, 29, 37, 43, 45, 46, 50, 51, 55, 56, 59, 63, 71, 74, 152, 154, 159
  auditory, 95, 96, 100
  brain, 22, 28, 33, 42, 45, 46, 70, 79, 158
  child/childhood, 20, 37, 42, 54, 65, 75, 78, 99, 105
  mental, 42, 43, 79, 115
  motor, viii, 20, 42, 46, 63, 69, 70, 72, 80, 152, 163
  neural, 20, 22, 47, 72, 80, 84, 105
  speech/language, viii, 4, 20, 52, 95, 98-100, 103
  visual, 106, 107, 113, 115, 150, 163
Developmentally delayed, 27, 31, 97, 99
Developmental movement patterns, 46, 47, 65, 66, 141, 149, 163
Directionality, 110, 114, 153
Dopamine, 40, 72, 89
Double Doodle, 128, 145, 146
Drugs, 43, 85, 96, 122
Dyslexia, 47

E

Ear infection, 31, 79, 81, 96, 97
Education, vii, viii, 2, 3, 19, 25, 26, 31, 32, 34, 54, 97, 108, 149
Education through Music, 104, 153
Educational Kinesiology Foundation, 17, 35, 153
Electronic media, 30, 31, 33, 106
Elephant, 81-83, 101, 102
Embryo, 3, 20, 30, 43, 79, 84, 95
EMFs, 31
Emotion, 2, 26, 30, 44, 95, 115
Emotional, vi-viii, 20, 28, 31, 33, 39, 47, 49, 54, 72, 80, 81, 84, 85, 87, 90, 92, 104, 120-122, 126, 130, 150, 152, 154, 159
Encouragement, 20, 23, 56, 75, 110, 124-126, 156
Environment, vi, 19, 21-24, 27, 28, 30, 32, 61, 69, 70, 72, 75, 77, 98, 104, 107, 110, 127, 149, 160
Environmental, 19-20, 31, 32, 43, 59, 93, 96
Evolving Art, 7, 9, 10
Exercise, 21, 33, 37, 39, 120, 153
Eye contact, 27, 48, 58, 126, 130, 142, 144
Eye-foot coordination, 69, 113
Eye-hand coordination, 7, 11, 15, 55, 66, 69, 71, 112, 113
Eye Rolls, 114
Eyes, 1, 11, 22, 24, 33, 34, 39, 43, 48, 58, 59, 77, 93, 105-119, 126, 145, 148, 153, 156
Eyes closed, 39, 40, 57, 59, 81, 91, 93, 94, 105, 114
Eyestrain, 106, 109
Eye movement, 7, 24, 62, 71, 80, 107, 108, 114
Eye teaming, 7, 58, 82, 106, 108, 116
Eye tracking, 7, 111

F

Facial nerves, 58
Failure syndrome, 124
Fear Paralysis reflex, 47

Fetus, 2, 3, 20, 30, 43, 48, 70, 79, 84,
 95, 96, 102, 103
Fight-or-flight, 29
Fluorescent lights, 31
Frontal sinuses, 119
Frontalis muscle, 119
Frontal lobes, 106, 119, 155

G

Gastrocnemius, 53
Genes, 19-21, 28, 91
Genetics, 19
Gibberish, 122
Giraffe, 37, 39
Gorilla Thump, 37, 41
Grasp reflex patterns, 12, 47, 52, 55
Gravity, 42, 51, 72, 78, 152
Grip, 7, 10, 12, 14, 55, 86, 128
Good Night Limbs, 67, 68, 131
Gustation, 78, 90

H

Hand-eye coordination, 66, 105, 106,
 150
Hearing, 3, 31, 34, 43, 46, 55, 64, 76-
 78, 82, 87, 95-100, 102, 104, 108,
 118, 124, 160
 impairment, 96, 97
Heart/heartbeat, 2, 3, 20, 22, 24, 26,
 30, 35-37, 71, 75, 86, 87, 89, 95,
 102, 103, 126, 127, 129, 159
Hemispheres, 8, 43, 46, 58, 65, 67, 82,
 155
Heredity, 19
Hippocampus, 21
Homolateral, 10, 66-69, 117
Homologous, 66-69, 117
Hook-ups, 35-37, 41, 81, 121, 122,
 141, 154-157
Hormones, 2, 20, 30, 50, 59
Human Sandwich, 86, 88
Hyperactivity, 27, 72, 85
Hypertension, 30
Hypothalamus, 91, 121
Hypotonic, 48, 49

I

Imagination, 9, 73-75, 100, 123, 125
Immune system, 41, 51, 84
In utero, viii, 2, 24, 46, 47, 54, 65, 70,
 79, 84, 87, 108
Indigo child/children, 25-27, 89
Infant, 4, 5, 24, 32, 42-47, 50, 51, 55,
 56, 59, 69, 70, 74, 79-81, 85, 87,
 97, 101, 107, 110, 113, 124, 138-
 140, 163
InfantSEE, 110
Infant Walker, 42, 43
Intelligence, 19, 47, 53, 115, 124, 133
Integration, 45, 46, 48, 51, 58, 69,
 111, 153
 sensory, 7, 42, 69, 72, 118, 158
Intuition, 5

K

Kindergarten, vii, 2, 3, 35, 100, 118,
 136, 150, 154, 158, 159

L

Language, viii, 4, 5, 18, 22, 47, 52, 58,
 76, 80, 81, 89, 95-100, 102-104,
 115, 123, 130
Laterality, 54, 64, 110, 143, 153
Lazy 8s, 7, 11, 12, 70, 112, 115, 117,
 139
Learning, vi, viii, 1-3, 15, 17-19, 21-23,
 29, 31-35, 38, 43, 44, 48, 50, 51,
 54, 56, 57, 61, 63, 64, 66, 68, 69,
 71, 72, 76, 80, 81, 84, 89, 97-99,
 104-109, 118, 121, 124, 129, 130,
 142, 146, 149, 150, 152-155,
 158-160
Learning pyramid, 54
Light sensitivity, 58
Locomotor, 43, 54, 75, 107
Loopty Loops, 7-9, 14

M

Marsden ball, 114
Massage, 4, 37, 134
Mathematics, 5, 83, 152

Memory, 3, 21, 38, 52, 55, 64, 94, 102, 111, 112, 121, 155, 158

Movement, viii, 1, 7, 11, 17, 19, 22-24, 29, 32, 33, 35, 36, 39, 42-47, 49, 50, 52, 55, 57, 59, 72, 74, 75, 78-82, 85, 90, 93, 94, 100, 102-105, 107, 108, 112, 114, 116-118, 134, 136, 141, 143-146, 150, 152-156, 158, 160, 163

Moro reflex, 47, 49, 51, 54, 95

Mouse Hunt for Cheese, 67

Mouthing, 65, 66, 68, 117

Music, 3, 32, 37, 73, 78, 95, 96, 100-104, 134, 136, 138, 140, 142, 156, 158

Myelinate, 20, 64, 91, 108

Myopia, 106, 115

N

Navel radiation, 65-68, 117

Neocortex, 20, 43, 46, 62, 67, 106, 155

Nervous system, 1, 4, 20, 22, 29, 31, 38, 41, 46, 64, 79, 80, 84, 88, 90, 93, 105, 150, 152

Neurons, 21-23, 90, 91, 93, 107, 108

Newborn, vii, 19, 24, 44, 46-49, 57, 70, 87, 97, 107

Nourishment, vii, 45, 47, 48, 65, 85, 97, 120

Now It's Time, 140

Nuchal cord, 48, 49

Nurture, 2, 3, 19, 24, 27, 28, 104

Nurturing Hands, 37, 39

Nutrition, 31, 35

O

Obstacle course, 70, 139

Ocular lock, 34

Olfactory perception, 91, 163

Ossicles, 95

Ouchy clearing, 122

Oxytocin, 48

Oxygen, 38, 39, 48, 96, 155

P

PACE, 35, 141, 154-156

Pencil grip, 7, 10, 12, 86

Penmanship, 7, 11, 14

Peripheral vision, 103, 113, 145

Personal Power Pose, 37, 40

Play, viii, 4-6, 12, 15, 22, 30, 33, 37, 40, 48, 53, 57, 60-63, 69-76, 87, 89, 93, 100, 101, 104-106, 111-113, 117-119, 129, 133-136, 138, 141, 142, 144, 146, 148, 151, 154, 158, 160, 163

Playpens, 42, 43

PLTs, 2, 31, 37, 55, 76, 158, 163

Positive Points, 119, 121, 122

Posture, 1, 17, 62

Potty training, 6, 52, 53

Pregnancy, 2, 19, 22, 37, 40, 43, 47, 50, 59, 96

Pregnant, 30, 43, 47, 70, 79, 96, 133

Primary Learning Tools, vi, vii, 2, 14, 31, 55, 56, 70, 76, 84, 152, 157, 158, 160, 163

Proprioception, 77, 78, 93, 94, 118, 143, 144, 163

R

Readiness, viii, 7, 35, 52, 142, 154

Reading, vii, 7, 18, 31-34, 38, 43, 51, 52, 54, 60, 67, 71, 76, 81, 83, 96-98, 100, 101, 105-107, 109, 118, 134, 136, 142, 145, 146, 152, 153

Reflex/Reflexes, 12, 45-55, 57, 59, 60, 65, 66, 68, 74, 80, 84, 90, 94. 95, 108, 116-118, 121, 127, 145, 152

Respect, 128-131, 151

Rhythm, 39, 49, 50, 56-58, 83, 102, 103, 117, 118

Rigid educational systems, 32

Running wheel, 21, 22

S

Seeing, 34, 55, 64, 105, 108, 109, 116, 146, 160

Self-esteem, 2, 124, 126, 127, 148
Smell, 24, 34, 77, 91-93, 118, 121
Smile Breathing, 37, 38
Snowballs, 7, 10
Sound, 4, 22, 23, 32, 41, 55, 56, 58,
    75, 78, 79, 93, 95, 96, 98-105, 151
Spatial awareness, 34, 82, 103, 145
Speech, vii, 4, 27, 31, 46, 55, 62, 65,
    76, 81, 89, 95-100
Spinal movement, 65, 66, 68
Spinal Galant reflex, 47, 48, 54
Spinal Pereze reflex, 47, 48, 54
Sports, vi, 32, 37, 50, 67, 69, 71, 105,
    145, 154, 159
Squeezies, 86, 116, 117
STAR testing, 17, 18
Stress, 2, 7, 19, 20, 27, 29-31, 34,
    36-39, 41, 43, 51, 53, 54, 130,
    154, 157
Sucking, 4, 47, 49, 50, 58, 59, 65, 68,
    94
SuperConfitelligent child, vi, 48, 159,
    160, 163
Swaddling, 86, 87

T

33 Ways to Encourage a Child©, 125
Tactile Embrace®, 86
Tactilely defensive, 84
Talking hand motions, 7, 12, 13
Taste perception, 91, 163
Teachable minutes, 3, 5, 24
Television, vii, 2, 14, 30, 33-35, 72,
    98, 105
Tendon Guard reflex, 53
Tension Tamers, 37, 163
Terrible Twos, 131
Terrific Twos, 131
Thinking Caps, 101, 102, 156
TMJ, 4
Toe walking, 5
Touch, 7, 22, 41, 44, 46, 49, 59, 71, 76,
    77, 79, 84-90, 93, 107, 113, 114,
    117, 118, 122, 126, 138, 163

Trimester, 48, 95
Tracking, 7, 108, 111, 113-116
Tummy Time, 23, 56

V

Vaccines, 32, 33
Vestibular, 15, 31, 46, 47, 49, 69, 74,
    76-81, 83-85, 102, 105, 108, 116,
    118, 143, 144, 150, 152, 155, 158,
    163
Visual
    acuity, 106, 108, 113, 116
    closure, 111
    constancy, 111
    discrimination, 55, 110, 111, 145
    figure ground discrimination, 111
    form recognition, 111
    integration, 110, 112
    midfield, 115
    motor activities, 115, 163
    motor integration, 81, 108, 112,
        116, 150
    perception, 74, 105, 109, 110, 163
    sequential memory, 112
    spatial sub-skills, 110
    spatial memory, 111
    speed and span of perception, 112
Visualization, 112, 143

W

Walking, 39, 43, 50, 51, 59, 62, 67, 69-
    71, 80, 81, 93, 94, 102, 111, 138
Water, vii, 6, 15, 21, 31, 37-39, 57, 58,
    68, 73, 74, 90, 93, 101, 112, 134,
    141, 154, 155
WBCH©, 154-156, 159, 163
Wernicke's Area, 55
Whole-brain, 1, 8, 130, 153, 156
Writing, 7, 9, 11, 14, 32, 51, 52, 54, 60,
    67, 71, 76, 81, 86, 100, 105, 127,
    136, 142, 143, 145, 146, 152, 153,
    163

X

X Marks the Spot, 116-118

Author Biography

Denise Hornbeak has been in the educational and holistic health fields since 1977 and is one of the pioneers of the Brain Gym® program. Denise has consulted, designed and implemented inservice programs for numerous school districts from preschool through the postgraduate level. She has presented at the Annual CA Regional Vision Therapy Forum, READ Annual Tutor Conference and many Whole Life Expos.

Over the years Denise has worked with children from a few weeks old to severely disabled elderly. She has experience with specialty populations such as those with brain injury/trauma, neurological imbalances, learning disabilities, ADD/ADHD, the autism spectrum, developmentally delayed challenges, and visual and auditory impairment. In her private practice she has taken slow learners who are getting low or failing grades and often labeled lazy or dyslexic and watched them turn around to being highly motivated outstanding students.

Denise implements such modalities as Neurokinesiology, Touch for Health®, Brain Gym®, Educational Kinesiology, Heartmath®, Natural Vision Techniques, Phototherapy® and Bal-A-Vis-X®. She brings a compassionate approach to mind, body and spirit to her private practice. Denise provides a relaxed and safe learning environment for children and adults to be themselves, make mistakes without fear and draw out their own innate potential.

Denise received her undergraduate degree in Psychology with a minor in Special Education from the University of Maine in Orono and her M.S. (Master of Science in Health and Human Service) from Columbia Commonwealth University. She is a Licensed Educational Kinesiologist (L.E.K.), a Natural Vision Trainer (N.V.T.) and a Color Light Practitioner (C.L.P.).

"There are few things more rewarding than watching an insecure individual with low self-esteem blossom into a self-confident person with a sparkle in their eyes."

— Denise C. Hornbeak